Edited by Jim Heimann with
an introduction by Steve Heller

The Golden Age of Advertising – the 70s

TASCHEN

KÖLN LONDON LOS ANGELES MADRID PARIS TOKYO

Steven Heller:

Alcohol &
Tobacco
16

Automobiles
46

Business &
Industry
84

Consumer
Products
102

Entertainment
168

Fashion &
Beauty
206

Food &
Beverage
266

RICAN

Travel
324

Interiors
296

The Seventies
Not Quite the Sixties

by Steven Heller

Sixties movies, music, art, and advertising were infinitely more innovative than seventies fare in every way. Such high points as disco, glam rock, The Village People, *Dirty Harry*, *Love Story*, and *The Brady Bunch*® notwithstanding, the seventies were a cultural sinkhole, and this goes triple for print advertising, which reflected at least some of the zeitgeist. The collective American memory may vividly recall a decade of great ad campaigns and slogans, memorable jingles, and cute trade mascots, but television was its medium, not print. There were many great commercials playing on all three U. S. networks—and devoted Americans watched them day and night, night and day.

To wit: Budweiser's® omnipresent "This Bud's for you," McDonald's® "You deserve a break today at McDonald's," Burger King's® "Have it your way," Merrill Lynch's® "Merrill Lynch is Bullish on America," and kosher frank manufacturer Hebrew National's® "We answer to a higher authority." These and other brilliant slogans were such potent verbal weapons that media buyers bought huge blocks of time in order to repeat the commercials over and over on each network, forever embedding these pearls into the consumer's

malleable mind. Such invasive messages captured the public's consciousness, while the print versions for many of the same products were often uninspired.

Of course, there were exceptions to the rule like "The Jordache® Look", which started the denim revolution when it was launched on TV and continued its fetching foray into semi-nude exhibitionism through magazines and billboards across the nation, circa 1979. For the most part, however, watching real actors and hearing real voice-overs, like the dulcet-toned narrator for BMW's® 1975 "The ultimate driving machine," brought shrewd slogans to life in more seductive ways. Even the most annoying of commercial slogans—"Ladies, please don't squeeze the Charmin®!" (Benton & Bowles' brainchild that launched in 1964, but continued ad nauseam throughout the seventies)—was far more effective when seen on the small screen than in lackluster print equivalents.

During the fifties and sixties, print art directors were the advertising industry's luminaries. These masters of "creative" designed the memorably beautiful ads of the era. Back then, high-circulation national magazines such as *Look*, *Life*, *Collier's*, and *The Saturday Evening Post* were stuffed with multitudinous pages. Advertising art directors competed with editorial designers to see who could make the most conceptually startling and typographically attractive pages, and there was no paucity of "Big Ideas" in the art directors' annuals. Television, however, was another story.

Although TV began to reach large audiences in the late fifties and early sixties, advertising agencies had not yet translated the revolutionary "Big Idea" strategy from the page to the screen. Most commercials had a tentative, even amateurish, tenor until the mid-sixties, when major advertising dollars were pulled from behemoth magazines and diverted to the newer form. General magazines simply carried too much overhead to be cost-effective and, with larger numbers of readers than their ad revenues could effi-

ciently support, most began to fold. Having ceased to be magnets for mass-market national campaigns, *Collier's* and *The Saturday Evening Post* were the first to fail; *Look* followed after an admirable push to modernize; and *Life* ultimately succumbed to the ad drain, initially reducing to a monthly circulation and eventually ceasing altogether. Meanwhile, leading brands massively invested in prime airtime, thus siphoning off the agencies' top ad executives from print to TV. The bar was rapidly raised for one medium and incrementally lowered for the other, which ultimately had a discernible impact on the disparate quality of the talent pool between the two classes of art directors.

A sea change in the late sixties grew into a tidal wave by the early seventies, with certain stylistic mannerisms also being washed away. Initially, print advertising looked toward editorial design as a model. Typographic sophistication was at a high level, but soon print turned into a mélange of editorial and TV sensibilities. Consciously or not, the cathode ray screen rather than the magazine page became the new design paradigm, and the short attention span of its audience became that of the new reader. Where once-generous margins of white space framed clever head-lines and photographs, in the seventies full-page photographs filled the entire page and headlines were dropped willynilly onto the pictures. Advertisements like "Feel Clean All Over" (p. 308), hawking the benefits of gas heat, used colorful, tightly cropped photo-graphs to hit the viewer between the eyes, just like on TV—which is exactly where that campaign began.

Print had its own requisites, but innova-tion appeared to be less important than the status quo. An ad for the new, subcompact Honda Civic®—headlined "Women only drive automatic transmissions" (p. 308), an ironic pseudo-feminist concept—recalled the look of the great era of the Doyle Dane Bernbach® (DDB) Volkswagen Beetle® ads. Conversely, the text for VW's own "Volkswagen Does It Again," hawking its new Rabbit®, did not live up to the refined copy of its predecessors. While this late-model VW ad attempted to reprise the same witty tone of the earlier classic campaigns (showing that a seven-foot-one-inch NBA legend, Wilt Chamberlain, could easily fit into the subcompact car), it was a smaller idea than the famous "Lemon" ad that

pioneered the use of irony to make VW an acceptable, sought-after, alternative driving machine for gas-guzzling Americans.

During the sixties, inventive (often sur-real) photography had eclipsed realistic illustration as the visual red meat of print advertising, an aesthetic that was carried through into the seventies. By this time, however, audiences were becoming condi-tioned to the flow of images on TV and seemed to have less patience for the static picture. So the photographic nuance and subtlety common to fifties and sixties print ads were overshadowed in their turn by unambiguous studio reality. The photograph of a beautiful AfricanAmerican woman for Kent® cigarettes (p. 35) stares passively but unambiguously at the viewer. While this ad was significant for its employ of a black fash-ion model, the "I Want You" style was also notable because it was a standard manner of complementing a persuasive TV barrage. Of course, there were also exceptions to the typ-ical photographs: in one of the most arrest-ing ads, Time Inc.'s "As long as the still pic-ture can move... we're in the right business," a dramatic photograph of U. S. Army troops carrying a wounded comrade off the battle-

field defiantly shows the power of the frozen moment. This ad made a convincing case, but few other print advertisements were so effective.

Illustration made a minor comeback in the seventies, but the result was often styl-ized and decorative rather than intellectual and conceptual. The illustration for Clairol's® ad announcing its first foray into herbal essence shampoos was an appropriate use of a light-hearted, fairy-tale style, but did not challenge the perceptions of its audience in the same way as the classic Miss Clairol ("Does She... or Doesn't She?") back in 1959. Likewise, the sprightly-looking ad for Alcoa Aluminum borrows the linear quality, color palette, and radical psychedelic style of the progressive Push Pin Studios, yet reduces the form to cutesy insignificance. When irony is absent, what results is safe... which is not to say that all commercial advertising should be so bold and revolutionary—after all, grab-bing attention by whatever means is the ultimate goal, and imparting a positive mes-sage outweighs all other purposes. Yet sev-enties' practice relied on the tried-and-true rather than the challenging and new.

Advertising historians note that the decade marked a period when slavish ad-herence to market testing and focus groups reigned. Advertising and brand development were becoming too competitively risky to be left to chance. In order to determine the effectiveness of TV and print promotion, the agencies relied on focus groups, which often had a say in altering (or mutilating) cam-paigns to conform to mass opinion. While certain firms—like DDB; Ammirati Puris; Foote, Cone & Belding; Lord, Geller, Federico, Einstein; and George Lois—retained enough creative influence to overcome the mass dumbing-down with the products they han-dled, other less-established or more mass-market agencies acceded to the will of the focus experts. And it was easy to spot the lesser lights. Advertisements that packed too much into a page, like "Sisters are differ-ent from brothers," for African-American hair products, were doubtless the result of

too many focus sessions and committee decisions.

The seventies constituted a wellspring of a different sort, however. It was the decade when natural product lines, including shampoos and foods, were first advertised on a national stage. Racial and ethnic barriers were also falling rapidly. While different groups were targeted with distinct "ethnic" campaigns, African Americans and other "minorities" were participating more in general advertising, which led to more integrated commercials in the eighties. There was a further significant milestone: cigarette TV commercials were banned in the seventies, relegating tobacco advertisements exclusively to print until they, too, were censored in the nineties.

The purpose of advertising is to serve clients in their quest for profit; it was never intended as an engine for culture. It is therefore unrealistic to expect the majority of ads in any period to transcend this basic function. At certain points in history, however, owing to the creative force of brilliantly artistic and driven people, advertising has defined the cultural gestalt every bit as much as music, film, and literature; more frequently,

it has incorporated and mainstreamed certain elements of these. Even the most progressive aspects of advertising build upon other cultural foundations. Avant-gardes, for example, are drafted into service by advertising agencies only after they have become more or less mainstream. It is therefore the job of an acute advertising executive to determine when to start riding the wave of a unique phenomenon, before it crests. He or she must also know the media that will best serve as a vehicle for such a ride. During the seventies, creative teams pumped out thousands of ads and commercials, but print was no longer the best means by which to reach a mass audience, magazines having become more specialized.

To survive in a competitive market, magazines had to target smaller niche groups of focused consumers, which certainly appealed to advertisers. While major brands continued to follow traditional advertising formulas and built campaigns around TV exposure, this new strategy of specialization forced reevaluation. Even in print advertising, the clients demanded more vitality to increase their fortunes. So, despite this essay's lament of the dearth of creativity, print advertising was

poised to recoup some of its losses through placement in a host of smaller venues. This, in turn, helped launch a revival of more ambitious and inventive approaches in the eighties and nineties—a time, incidentally, when regulations and taboos about content in advertising were being reevaluated once again.

Steven Heller is art director of the *New York Times* Book Review and co-chair of the MFA/Design program at the School of Visual Arts. He is also the author and editor of over eighty books on graphic design and popular culture, including *The Graphic Design Reader, Paul Rand, From Merz to Emigre and Beyond: Avant-Garde Magazine Design of the 20th Century,* and *Citizen Design: Perspectives on Design Responsibility.*

Die Siebziger:
Fast so gut wie die Sechziger

von Steven Heller

In den Sechzigern waren Film, Musik, Kunst und Werbung in jeder Hinsicht innovativer als in den Siebzigern. Trotz Highlights wie Disco, Glamrock, Village People, *Dirty Harry*, *Love Story* und *The Brady Bunch®* waren die Jahre von 1970 bis 1980 eine kulturelle Talsohle sondergleichen, was doppelt und dreifach für die Printwerbung gilt, wodurch sich aber wenigstens den Zeitgeist widerspiegelt. Das kollektive amerikanische Gedächtnis mag sich lebhaft an ein Jahrzehnt großartiger Werbekampagnen, einprägsamer Slogans und süßer Werbefiguren erinnern – das Medium dieser Dekade war das Fernsehen, nicht das gedruckte Wort. Viele hervorragende Werbespots liefen auf allen drei großen amerikanischen Sendern gleichzeitig und ihre treuen Fans sahen sie sich Tag für Tag an.

Ich denke dabei an den allgegenwärtigen Budweiser®-Slogan „This Bud's for you", McDonald's® „You deserve a break today at McDonald's", die Sprüche von Burger King® „Have it your way" und Merrill Lynch® „Merrill Lynch is Bullish on America" oder an Hebrew National®, den Hersteller koscherer Würstchen, der mit „We answer to a higher authority" warb. Die Werbeabteilungen

kauften große Zeitblöcke, um die Spots auf allen Sendern ständig zu wiederholen. So prägten diese allgegenwärtigen Werbespots das Bewusstsein der breiten Öffentlichkeit, während die gedruckten Versionen, die oft für dieselben Produkte warben, von wenig Inspiration zeugten.

Natürlich gab es Ausnahmen von dieser Regel, wie die Kampagne „The Jordache® Look", mit deren Fernsehausstrahlung die Jeansrevolution eingeleitet wurde. Meist wirkten raffinierte Slogans jedoch verführerischer, wenn echte Schauspieler zu sehen und echte Stimmen zu hören waren, wie die sonore Erzählerstimme in der BMW®-Werbung von 1975: „The ultimate driving machine." Selbst nervtötende Werbesprüche wie „Ladies, please don't squeeze the Charmin®!" (diese Toilettenpapierwerbung, Kopfgeburt von Benton & Bowles, kam 1964 heraus, lief aber die gesamten Siebziger hindurch weiter, bis sie niemand mehr hören konnte) wirkten auf der Mattscheibe wesentlich ansprechender als in den langweilig gestalteten Anzeigen.

In den fünfziger und sechziger Jahren waren die Artdirectors aus dem Printbereich die Stars der Werbebranche. Diese Topkreativen entwarfen die schönen und unvergesslichen Anzeigen jener Ära. Damals hatten die großen Zeitschriften *Look*, *Life*, *Collier's* und *The Saturday Evening Post* hohe Auflagen und unglaublich viele Seiten. Die Kreativdirektoren aus der Werbeabteilung lagen mit den Leuten vom redaktionellen Layout im Wettstreit, wer die konzeptionell und typografisch attraktivsten Seiten gestalten konnte. Im TV-Bereich sah es jedoch noch ganz anders aus.

In den USA erreichte das Fernsehen ab den späten Fünfzigern ein Massenpublikum, doch die Werbeagenturen hatten es noch nicht geschafft, die revolutionäre Strategie der „Big Idea", der zentralen Werbebotschaft, von der gedruckten Seite auf den Bildschirm zu übertragen. Das Werbefernsehen hatte bis Mitte der sechziger Jahre einen zögerlichen, ja amateurhaften Charakter, doch dann wurde schließlich ein Großteil der Werbedollars aus den monströs dicken Zeitschriften abgezo-

gen und in das neue Medium gesteckt. Viele Zeitschriften hatten zu hohe laufende Kosten, um rentabel zu sein, und die meisten mussten ihr Erscheinen einstellen. *Collier's* und *The Saturday Evening Post* gingen als Erste ein; *Look* folgte nach einem bewundernswerten Versuch der Modernisierung, und *Life* fiel schließlich ebenfalls dem Inseratschwund zum Opfer, nachdem sie zunächst statt wöchentlich nur noch monatlich erschienen war. Währenddessen investierten die führenden Marken in Werbeblöcke zur besten Sendezeit, was zu einer Abwanderung der führenden Köpfe der Werbeagenturen vom Druckbereich zum Fernsehen führte. Die Ansprüche in dem einen Medium stiegen schnell, während sie in dem anderen immer niedriger wurden.

Was Ende der Sechziger noch eine allmähliche Wandlung gewesen war, wuchs Anfang der Siebziger zu einer wahren Flutwelle der Veränderung an, in deren Verlauf auch gewisse stilistische Eigenheiten verloren gingen. Der Standard in der Typografie war hoch, doch bald setzte sich auch in den Druckerzeugnissen eine Mischung aus Ansprüchen des Grafikdesigns und des Fernsehens durch. Die Mattscheibe wurde zum neuen gestalterischen Paradigma, die Zeitschriftenseite hatte ausgedient und die Aufmerksamkeitsspanne des neuen Lesers wurde so kurz wie die des Fernsehzuschauers. Wo früher großzügige weiße Ränder clevere Überschriften und Fotos umrahmt hatten, füllten in den Siebzigern großformatige Fotos die gesamte Seite, die Schriftzüge wurden einfach irgendwo auf das Bild geklatscht. Werbekampagnen wie „Feel Clean All Over" (S. 308) setzten bunte, knapp beschnittene Fotos ein, die den Betrachter wie ein Faustschlag trafen, genau wie im Fernsehen — wo die Kampagne natürlich auch herkam.

Der Druckbereich hatte seine eigenen Anforderungen, doch Innovation schien dort weniger wichtig zu sein als Aufrechterhaltung des Status quo. Eine Anzeige für den neuen Kleinwagen Honda Civic® mit dem äußerst ironischen, pseudofeministischen Slogan „Women only drive automatic transmissions" (S. 83) erinnerte an die große Ära der Anzeigen von Doyle Dane Bernbach® (DDB) für den VW Käfer®. Der Text, mit dem VW seinen neuen Rabbit® bewarb – „Volkswagen Does It Again" – erreichte nicht das hohe Niveau seiner Vorgänger. Diese Werbung versuchte zwar, den geistreichen Tonfall der legendären früheren Kampagnen zu treffen (hier wurde gezeigt, mit welcher Leichtigkeit die 2,13 Meter große Basketball-Legende Wilt Chamberlain in dem Kleinwagen Platz fand), war von der Idee her jedoch wesentlich blasser als die berühmte „Lemon"-Werbung. In dieser Werbung wurde zum ersten Mal Ironie eingesetzt, um den VW zu einer akzeptablen, ja begehrten Alternative für die Benzin saufenden amerikanischen Straßenkreuzer zu machen.

In den Sechzigern hatten einfallsreiche (oft surreale) Fotos realistische Zeichnungen als visuellen Hauptbestandteil der Printwerbung ersetzt, eine Ästhetik, die auch in den Siebzigern weitergeführt wurde. Zu diesem Zeitpunkt waren die Zuschauer jedoch bereits an den ständigen Wechsel der Bilder im Fernsehen gewöhnt und schienen nur noch wenig Geduld für das statische Foto aufzu-

bringen. Das führte dazu, dass die Subtilität der Werbefotografie in den fünfziger und sechziger Jahren der unzweideutigen Studiorealität weichen musste. In einer Anzeige für Kent®-Zigaretten (S. 35) starrt eine schöne afroamerikanische Frau den Betrachter passiv, aber völlig unzweideutig an. Diese Anzeige war insofern wichtig, als sie ein schwarzes Fotomodell zeigte; der „I Want You"-Stil war die Standardantwort auf das Werbefernseh-Bombardement. Es gab natürlich auch Ausnahmen von den stereotypen Fotos: Eine der bemerkenswertesten Anzeigen, die Time-Inc.-Werbung „As long as the still picture can move ... we're in the right business", zeigt ein dramatisches Foto amerikanischer Soldaten, die einen verwundeten Kameraden vom Schlachtfeld tragen, ein Bild, das trotzig die Überzeugungskraft des eingefrorenen Augenblicks unter Beweis stellt. Diese Anzeige vermittelte eine einprägsame Botschaft.

Illustrationen erlebten in den Siebzigern ein kleines Comeback, waren jedoch oft eher stilisiert und dekorativ als intellektuell oder konzeptionell. Die Zeichnungen in der Clairol®-Werbung, mit der das erste Kräutershampoo eingeführt wurde, setzten den verspielt-märchenhaften Stil zwar angemes-

sen ein, forderten die Intelligenz des Publikums aber nicht in gleicher Weise heraus, wie es die klassische Miss Clairol 1959 noch getan hatte („Does She ... or Doesn't She?"). Die spritzig aussehenden Anzeigen für Alcoa Aluminum liehen sich die grafische Qualität, Farbpalette und den radikal psychedelischen Stil der progressiven Push Pin Studios aus, reduzierten sie jedoch auf niedliche Bedeutungslosigkeit: Fehlt die Ironie, tut das Ergebnis niemandem weh. Was nicht heißen soll, dass alle kommerzielle Werbung mutig und revolutionär sein muss – oberstes Ziel ist es, Aufmerksamkeit zu erregen und eine positive Aussage zu vermitteln, gleichgültig mit welchen Mitteln. In der Praxis setzte man in den Siebzigern jedoch lieber auf Altbewährtes als auf Innovation.

Werbehistoriker wissen, dass in diesem Jahrzehnt ein sklavischer Glaube an Meinungsumfragen und Zielgruppen herrschte. Um die Wirksamkeit von Fernseh- und Printwerbung zu ermitteln, stützten die Werbeagenturen sich auf bestimmte Zielgruppen, die oft ihren Anteil an der Abwandlung (oder Verstümmelung) von Kampagnen hatten, um sie dem Massengeschmack entsprechend anzupassen. Während gewisse Werbefirmen

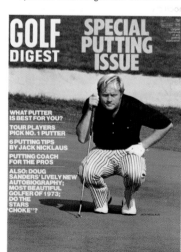

wie DDB, Ammirati Puris, Foote, Cone & Belding, Lord, Geller, Federico, Einstein und George Lois genug kreativen Einfluss behielten, um sich der Verdummung der von ihnen betreuten Produkte zu widersetzen, unterwarfen sich weniger etablierte Agenturen dem Willen der Marktforschung. Die kleineren Lichter sind leicht zu erkennen. Anzeigen, die zu viel auf einer Seite unterzubringen versuchten, wie „Sisters are different from brothers" für afroamerikanische Haarpflegeprodukte waren zweifelsohne das Resultat zu vieler Marktforscherei.

In anderer Hinsicht stellten die Siebziger allerdings einen Jungbrunnen neuer Ideen dar. Es war das Jahrzehnt, in dem Naturprodukte sowie Shampoos und Nahrungsmittel zum ersten Mal USA-weit vermarktet wurden. Auch ethnische Schranken fielen rasch. Während stark eingegrenzte Zielgruppen mit eindeutig „ethnischen" Kampagnen angesprochen wurden, waren Afroamerikaner und andere „Minderheiten" häufiger in der allgemeinen Werbung zu sehen, was zu der ethnisch integrierten Werbung der Achtziger führte. Einen weiteren wichtigen Meilenstein stellte das Verbot der Zigarettenwerbung im Fernsehen dar; der Tabakindustrie blieb nur noch die Printwerbung, bis auch diese in den Neunzigern verboten wurde.

Werbung wird zum Zweck der Gewinnmaximierung gemacht; sie war nie als kulturelle Triebkraft gedacht. Die Erwartung, dass der größere Teil der Werbung über diese Basisfunktion hinausgeht, ist daher zu jeder Zeit unrealistisch. In gewissen Sternstunden beeinflusst die Werbung allerdings Dank der Kreativität brillanter Künstler die Gesamtkultur nicht minder stark als Musik, Film und Literatur. Meistens vereinnahmt die Werbung jedoch gewisse Aspekte der Kultur für sich und schleust sie in den Zeitgeist ein. Selbst in ihren progressivsten Momenten bedient sich die Werbung immer bei anderen kulturellen Erscheinungen. Avantgardebewegungen werden beispielsweise erst dann von Werbeagenturen benutzt, wenn sie mehr oder minder Allgemeingut geworden sind. Aufgabe wacher Werbefachleute ist daher zu entscheiden, wann sie auf der Welle eines bestimmten Phänomens reiten sollen, bevor dieses seinen Höhepunkt überschritten hat. Sie müssen außerdem entscheiden, welches Medium das beste Vehikel für diesen Wellenritt abgeben wird. In den Siebzigern produzierten kreative Teams tausende von Anzeigen und Werbespots, doch Druckerzeugnisse waren nicht mehr die beste Methode, um das Massenpublikum zu erreichen.

Um sich auf einem hart umkämpften Markt behaupten zu können, mussten die Zeitschriften sich auf Spezialinteressen konzentrieren, was allerdings ganz im Sinne der Werbeindustrie war. Während die großen Marken weiterhin bei den altbewährten Rezepten blieben und ihre Kampagnen auf stetiger TV-Präsenz aufbauten, verlangte die Spezialisierung im Zeitschriftenbereich nach ganz neuen Strategien. Insgesamt gelang es der Printwerbung jedoch – trotz des in diesem Essay beklagten Verlusts ihrer Kreativität –, einige ihrer Defizite durch Platzierung in einer Vielzahl kleinerer Publikationen wieder wettzumachen. Das wiederum schuf die Ausgangsbasis für die Wiederbelebung anspruchsvollerer und innovativerer Ansätze in den Achtzigern und Neunzigern – eine Zeit, in der sich viele gesetzliche Vorschriften und Tabus in Bezug auf Werbeinhalte änderten.

Steven Heller ist Artdirector der *New York Times Book Review* und Vorsitzender der Fakultät Gestaltung (MFA/Design) an der School of Visual Arts in New York. Er ist außerdem Autor und Herausgeber von mehr als 80 Büchern über Grafikdesign und Populärkultur, u. a. *The Graphic Design Reader, Paul Rand, From Merz to Emigre and Beyond: Avant-Garde Magazine Design of the 20th Century* und *Citizen Design: Perspectives on Design Responsibility*.

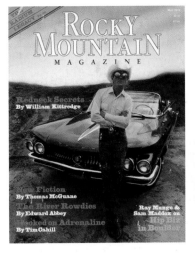

Käfer, Rabbit und Volkswagen sind eingetragene Marken der Volkswagenwerk Aktiengesellschaft.
BMW ist eine eingetragene Marke der Bayerischen Motoren Werke Aktiengesellschaft.
The Brady Bunch ist eine eingetragene Marke der Paramount Picture Corp.
Budweiser ist eine eingetragene Marke der Anheuser-Busch, Inc.
Burger King ist eine eingetragene Marke der Burger King Brands, Inc.
Charmin ist eine eingetragene Marke der Procter & Gamble Co.
Clairol ist eine eingetragene Marke der Clairol Inc.
Doyle Dane Bernbach ist eine eingetragene Marke der Omnicom International Holdings Inc.
Foote, Cone & Belding ist eine eingetragene Marke der Interpublic Group of Companies, Inc.
Hebrew National ist eine eingetragene Marke der ConAgra Brands, Inc.
Honda und Civic sind eingetragene Marken der Honda Motor Co.
Jordache ist eine eingetragene Marke der Jordache Enterprises, Inc.
Kent ist eine eingetragene Marke der Lorillard Licensing Co., L.L.C.
McDonald's ist eine eingetragene Marke der McDonald's Corp.
Merrill Lynch ist eine eingetragene Marke der Merrill Lynch & Co., Inc.
NBA ist eine eingetragene Marke der NBA Properties, Inc.

Les années 70 :
pas tout à fait les années 60

de Steven Heller

Le cinéma, la musique, l'art et la publicité des années 60 furent, à tous les égards, plus féconds que ceux des années 70. En dépit de points forts comme le disco, le glam-rock, les Village People, *L'inspecteur Harry*, *Love Story* et *The Brady Bunch*®, les années 70 furent un gouffre culturel, particulièrement dans le domaine de la publicité imprimée, reflet partiel de l'esprit d'une époque. Certes, au cours de cette décennie, de belles campagnes, de bons slogans, des jingles efficaces, de craquantes mascottes de marque ont laissé leur empreinte dans la mémoire collective américaine, mais leur vecteur était la télévision, pas le papier. De nombreuses pubs excellentes passaient sur les trois grandes chaînes nationales, que les fidèles téléspectateurs américains regardaient jour et nuit.

Pour n'en citer que quelques-unes : Budweiser® avec son omniprésent : « Cette Bud est pour toi » ; McDonald® : « Vous avez mérité une pause aujourd'hui chez McDonald » ; Burger King® : « Prenez-le comme vous voudrez » ; Merrill Lynch® : « Merrill Lynch remonte les bretelles de l'Amérique ». Ces slogans brillants et bien d'autres s'avérèrent des armes si puissantes que les acheteurs de média investirent massivement dans des temps d'antenne afin de pouvoir rediffuser inlassablement leurs pubs sur les chaînes nationales, gravant à jamais ces perles dans l'esprit malléable du consommateur. Le grand public retint ces messages envahissants alors que, souvent, les versions imprimées correspondant aux mêmes produits étaient ternes.

Naturellement, il y eut des exceptions à la règle, comme l'alléchant « look Jordache® » qui, lors de son lancement à la télévision vers 1979, déclencha la révolution du jean avant de poursuivre avec succès son incursion dans la semi nudité dans les magazines et sur les panneaux d'affichage de tout le pays. Toutefois, la présence de vrais acteurs et de commentaires en voix off, comme celui du narrateur au timbre suave de la pub de 1975 de BMW® : « La quintessence de la machine à conduire », donnait plus de relief aux messages. Même les slogans les plus aga-

çants tels que celui pour le papier hygiénique Charmin® : « Mesdames, merci de ne pas froisser le Charmin® » (une idée de l'agence Benton & Bowles de 1964 mais répétée jusqu'à plus soif tout au long des années 70) étaient plus efficaces à la télévision.

Au cours des années 50 et 60, les directeurs artistiques étaient les vraies sommités de la publicité imprimée. Ces maîtres de la « créativité » conçurent les belles et mémorables pubs de cette époque. Les magazines nationaux à grande diffusion tels que *Look*, *Life*, *Collier's* et *The Saturday Evening Post* étaient truffés d'innombrables annonces. Les directeurs artistiques publicitaires rivalisaient avec les graphistes et les maquettistes de ces revues pour créer les pages les plus saisissantes au niveau du concept et les plus séduisantes au niveau de la typographie. Ils ne manquaient pas alors de « grandes idées », et ce n'était pas le cas à la télévision.

Cette dernière commença à toucher de vastes audiences dès la fin des années 50 et au début des années 60, mais les agences de pub ne surent pas tout de suite transposer leur stratégie révolutionnaire de la « grande idée » de la page à l'écran. La plupart des spots conservèrent un côté hésitant,

amateur même, jusqu'au milieu des années 60, date à laquelle les gros budgets publicitaires furent détournés des magazines au profit du nouveau média. Les revues non spécialisées, écrasées par leurs frais généraux, n'étaient plus rentables. Ayant cessé d'attirer les campagnes nationales destinées au marché de masse, *Collier's* et *The Saturday Evening Post* furent les premières à disparaître. *Look* suivit, malgré un formidable effort de modernisation. *Life* succomba à son tour, passant d'abord d'hebdomadaire à mensuel puis cessant définitivement de paraître. Entre-temps, les grandes marques avaient investi massivement dans les tranches horaires de grande écoute, débauchant les meilleurs cadres des agences de publicité qui travaillaient autrefois sur le support papier.

Ces premiers remous apparus dans les années 60 se convertirent en raz de marée au début des années 70, balayant au passage certains maniérismes stylistiques. Au début, la publicité imprimée s'inspirait du graphisme éditorial. La sophistication typographique était d'un niveau élevé mais des sensibilités télévisuelles ne tardèrent pas à l'influencer également. Consciemment ou pas, l'écran du poste de télévision supplanta la page comme modèle stylistique et la faible capacité de concentration du téléspectateur devint celle du nouveau lecteur des années 70. Là où, autrefois, de généreuses marges blanches encadraient des photos et des textes intelligents, la page se remplit d'images et de textes lâchés un peu n'importe comment dans la composition. Des pubs comme « Sentez-vous propre de partout » (p. 308), vantant les bienfaits du chauffage au gaz, utilisaient des photos censées frapper le lecteur entre les deux yeux, comme à la télé (où cette campagne avait précisément commencé).

La publicité imprimée avait ses propres exigences, mais le statut quo primait sur l'innovation. Une pub pour la nouvelle petite Honda Civic® proclamait : « Les femmes ne conduisent que des automatiques » (p. 83), un concept pseudo-féministe ironique rappelant le look de la grande époque des pubs de la Volkswagen Beetle® (la Coccinelle) par l'agence Doyle Dane Bernbach®. Inversement, le texte de la pub VW, « Volkswagen remet ça », vantant sa nouvelle Rabbit®, n'était pas à la hauteur de ceux de ses prédécesseurs. Si cette pub de VW tentait de renouer avec le ton spirituel des campagnes classiques antérieures, l'idée ne valait pas le célèbre « Citron » qui avait inauguré le recours à l'ironie pour faire de VW une automobile acceptable et désirable pour les Américains.

Au cours des années 60, une photographie ingénieuse (souvent surréaliste) avait éclipsé l'illustration réaliste dans la publicité imprimée, créant une esthétique qui perdura tout au long des années 70. Cependant, le public de plus en plus conditionné par le flot des images de la télévision, semblait moins patient devant une représentation statique. Les nuances et les subtilités photographiques qui étaient le propre des pubs imprimées des années 50 et 60 furent donc à leur tour éclipsées par la réalité sans ambiguïté du studio. Dans une pub pour les cigarettes Kent® (p. 35), un beau mannequin afro-américain fixe l'objectif d'une manière passive mais sans équivoque. Si cette pub a son

importance pour son recours à une femme noire, son style « coup de poing » est également intéressant parce qu'il complète le matraquage télévisuel. Naturellement, il y avait des exceptions. L'une des pubs les plus saisissantes, pour Time Inc., illustre le pouvoir d'un moment figé : « Tant qu'une image fixe peut faire bouger ... nous sommes sur la bonne voie », et l'on voit des soldats américains transportant un camarade blessé hors du champ de bataille. Mais si celle-ci est convaincante, peu de pubs imprimées furent aussi efficaces.

L'illustration fit un vague come-back dans les années 70, mais d'une manière souvent stylisée et décorative. La pub Clairol® annonçant la première incursion de la marque dans les shampoings à essences végétales adoptait un style approprié, léger, féerique, mais sans remettre en question les perceptions du public comme le faisait la pub classique de Miss Clairol de 1959 (« Le fait-elle ... ou ne le fait-elle pas ? ») De même, l'illustration pour Alcoa Aluminium emprunte la qualité linéaire, la palette de couleurs et le style psychédélique radical des studios progressistes Push Pin mais réduit la formule à une insignifiance mièvre. Lorsque l'ironie est absente, le résultat est sans risque. Ce qui ne signifie pas que toutes les publicités devraient être audacieuses et révolutionnaires. Après tout, le but ultime est de retenir l'attention par tous les moyens, et transmettre un message positif l'emporte sur tous les autres objectifs.

Les historiens de la publicité observent que les années 70 furent marquées par une adhérence servile aux études de marché et aux panels de consommateurs. La publicité et le développement des marques devenaient trop compétitifs pour être laissés au hasard. Afin de déterminer l'efficacité d'une campagne à la télévision ou dans les journaux, les agences se reposaient sur des groupes de discussions, qui intervenaient souvent en altérant (ou mutilant) les projets afin de les rendre conformes à l'opinion de masse. Si certaines firmes (comme DDB, Ammirati Puris, Foote, Cone & Belding, Lord, Geller,

Federico, Einstein et George Lois) conservaient assez d'influence créative sur les produits qu'on leur confiait pour surmonter ce nivellement par le bas, d'autres agences moins établies ou plus orientées vers le marché de masse se plièrent à la volonté des experts. Les pubs qui en mettaient trop sur la page, comme « Les sœurs sont différentes des frères », pour des produits capillaires, étaient généralement le produit de trop de réunions et de décisions.

Durant les années 70, les lignes de produits naturels, qu'il s'agisse de shampoings ou d'aliments, firent l'objet de campagnes nationales. Les barrières raciales et ethniques tombaient rapidement. Si les différents groupes continuaient à être ciblés avec des campagnes « ethniques » distinctes, les Afro-américains et d'autres « minorités » furent davantage inclus dans la publicité générale. Il y eut un autre virage important : vanter les mérites des cigarettes fut interdit à la télévision, reléguant les pubs au support papier jusqu'à ce que, là aussi, elles soient interdites dans les années 90.

L'objectif de la publicité est de servir les annonceurs dans leur quête de profits, elle n'a jamais eu pour but d'être un véhicule

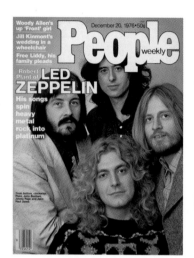

Steven Heller est directeur artistique du *New York Times Book Review* et codirecteur du programme MFA/Design de la School of Visual Arts. Il est également l'auteur et l'éditeur de plus de quatre-vingt livres sur le graphisme et la culture populaire, dont *The Graphic Design Reader, Paul Rand, From Merz to Emigre and Beyond : Avant-Garde Magazine Design of the 20th Century* et *Citizen Design : Perspectives on Design Responsibility*.

culturel. Il n'est donc pas réaliste d'attendre de la majorité des pubs qu'elles transcendent leur fonction de base. Néanmoins, à certaines époques, du fait de la créativité d'artistes inspirés, la publicité a contribué à modeler la culture au même titre que la musique, le cinéma et la littérature. Le plus souvent, elle a incorporé leurs éléments dans la culture de masse. Même dans ses aspects les plus progressistes, elle s'édifie sur d'autres bases culturelles. Les avant-gardes, par exemple, sont mobilisées par les agences publicitaires uniquement après avoir été plus ou moins digérées par le grand public. La mission d'un publicitaire de pointe est donc de déterminer à quel moment surfer sur la vague d'un phénomène unique avant qu'elle ne se brise. Il doit également savoir quel média offrira le véhicule le plus efficace pour un tel exercice. Au cours des années 70, les équipes créatives ont produit des milliers de pubs imprimées et de spots publicitaires, mais le papier n'était plus le meilleur support pour toucher un public de masse, les magazines étant devenus trop spécialisés.

Pour survivre sur un marché compétitif, les revues durent cibler des créneaux plus petits de consommateurs, ce qui n'était pas

pour déplaire aux publicistes. Tandis que les grandes marques continuaient d'appliquer les formules publicitaires traditionnelles et construisaient leurs campagnes autour d'une diffusion télévisuelle, cette nouvelle stratégie de spécialisation nécessita une réévaluation. Même dans la publicité imprimée, les annonceurs exigeaient plus de vitalité. Aussi, en dépit de mes lamentations sur la baisse de créativité dans cette introduction, la publicité imprimée était prête à récupérer une partie de ses pertes en réinvestissant dans une légion de projets plus petits. Ceci favorisa un regain d'approches plus ambitieuses et inventives dans les années 80 et 90, une époque où, d'ailleurs, les règles et les tabous sur le contenu en publicité devaient à nouveau être réévalués.

Los años setenta:

nada que ver con los sesenta

por Steven Heller

El cine, la música, la publicidad y el arte en los años sesenta fueron infinitamente más innovadores que en los setenta. Con las notables excepciones de la música disco, el glam rock, los Village People, *Harry el Sucio*, *Love Story* y *La tribu de los Brady*, la década de los setenta fue culturalmente yerma, en especial en cuanto a publicidad impresa se refiere, lo cual refleja en cierto modo el espíritu de los tiempos. Y aunque en la memoria colectiva de los norteamericanos pervive una década de grandes campañas y eslóganes publicitarios, de sintonías memorables y de graciosas mascotas comerciales, lo cierto es que todo eso tuvo lugar en el medio televisivo, no en prensa. Anuncios excelentes inundaban las parrillas de las tres cadenas de televisión de Estados Unidos y los norteamericanos permanecían devotamente frente a la pantalla día y noche, noche y día.

Entre las frases publicitarias más célebres se cuentan la omnipresente «Esta Bud es para ti», de Budweiser®; «Hoy usted se lo merece, venga a McDonald's», de McDonald's®; «A tu manera», de Burger King®; «Merrill Lynch, al alza en América», de la consultora financiera Merrill Lynch®, y «Respondemos a una autoridad superior», del fabricante de productos *kosher* Hebrew National®. Estos y otros eslóganes brillantes constituían armas verbales tan potentes que los anunciantes adquirieron enormes bloques de espacio televisivo para proyectarlos una y otra vez, hasta incrustar para siempre estas joyas en la mente maleable del consumidor. Y mientras que estos mensajes calaban en la conciencia del público, con frecuencia las versiones impresas de muchos de los mismos productos mostraban una carencia absoluta de inspiración.

Evidentemente, hubo excepciones, como por ejemplo la campaña de «El look Jordache®», que hacia 1979 inició la revolución de los vaqueros con su lanzamiento en televisión y continuó su seductor coqueteo con el semidesnudo en las páginas de las revistas y en las vallas publicitarias de todo Estados Unidos. Sin embargo, ver a actores de carne y hueso y oír sus voces superpuestas a las imágenes –como la del narrador de la campaña de BMW® que en 1975 incitaba con tono dulce al espectador a disfrutar de «El placer de conducir»– contribuía a que estos audaces eslóganes resultaran mucho más llamativos para el gran público. Incluso la más bochornosa de las frases publicitarias, «Por favor, no aprieten el Charmin®» (eslogan que Benton & Bowles acuñó en 1964 para anunciar su papel higiénico y que continuó explotando ad náuseam a lo largo de la década de los setenta) resultaba infinitamente más eficaz cuando se proyectaba en la pequeña pantalla que cuando aparecía en las deslucidas páginas de las revistas.

Durante los años cincuenta y sesenta, los directores de arte de la prensa se erigieron como las lumbreras de la industria publicitaria. Estos maestros de la «creatividad» diseñaron los memorables anuncios de una era. En aquella época, las revistas de amplia circulación nacional, como *Look*, *Life*, *Collier's* y *The Saturday Evening Post*, contaban con infinidad de páginas y los directores de arte publicitarios colaboraban con los diseñadores editoriales para crear las composiciones tipográficamente más atractivas y conceptualmente más sorprendentes. Por

entonces, los anuarios de los directores de arte jamás reflejaban una falta de «grandes ideas»; en cambio, la televisión era otra historia.

Cuando la televisión empezó a llegar al gran público a finales de los años cincuenta y principios de los sesenta, las agencias de publicidad aún no habían trasladado la revolucionaria estrategia de la «gran idea» de la página impresa a la pantalla. La mayor parte de los anuncios presentaba un corte vacilante, incluso *amateur*, hasta mediados de la década de los sesenta, cuando el dinero que se invertía en las voluminosas revistas empezó a desviarse al nuevo medio. Los gastos de las publicaciones empezaron a ser mayores que sus beneficios y muchas de ellas cerraron. Habiendo dejado de servir de imán para las campañas comerciales nacionales, las primeras en abdicar fueron *Collier's* y *The Saturday Evening Post*, a las que siguió *Look*, no sin antes realizar un admirable intento por modernizarse; finalmente, *Life* sucumbió a la sequía de publicidad y, tras reducir su circulación a una publicación mensual, acabó por cerrar sus puertas. Entre tanto, las grandes marcas invertían cantidades ingentes en las franjas horarias de máxima audiencia, desviando con ello a los mejores creativos publicitarios de la prensa a la televisión. Pronto, el baremo aumentó en un medio y descendió cada vez más en el otro, lo cual, en última instancia, tuvo un impacto ostensible en la calidad dispar de talento entre ambos tipos de directores de arte.

El cambio de oleaje de finales de los años sesenta se convirtió a principios de los setenta en una agitada marea que se llevó consigo todo rastro de peculiaridad estilística. En un principio, la publicidad impresa buscó en el diseño editorial un modelo a seguir. Y si bien la sofisticación tipográfica se hallaba en un momento álgido, las publicaciones no tardaron en transformarse en una mezcla de sensibilidades editoriales y televisivas. De manera consciente o inconsciente, la pantalla de rayos catódicos fue restando protagonismo a la página impresa como paradigma de diseño y el breve lapso

de atención de su audiencia pasó a sustituir al del lector. Los generosos márgenes blancos que otrora habían enmarcado ingeniosas frases publicitarias y deslumbrantes fotografías fueron reemplazados en los años setenta por imágenes a toda página en las cuales se insertaban los eslóganes de cualquier manera. Anuncios como «El calor limpio» (p. 308), que pregonaba los beneficios de la calefacción de gas, utilizaron fotografías a sangre y a todo color para atraer la mirada del espectador, imitando la técnica de la televisión, medio en el cual, por otro lado, se había iniciado la campaña.

Y aunque la prensa tenía sus propios requisitos, lo cierto es que la innovación parecía ser menos importante que el statu quo. Un anuncio del nuevo utilitario Honda Civic®–cuyo titular rezaba «Las mujeres sólo conducen transmisiones automáticas» (p. 83), un irónico concepto pseudofeminista– retomaba el aspecto de la gran era de los anuncios del Escarabajo® de Volkswagen creados por Doyle Dane Bernbach® (DDB). No obstante, el eslogan «Volkswagen vuelve a hacerlo», con el que se presentaba el nuevo Rabbit®, no tenía ni punto de comparación con sus refinados antecesores. Así,

aunque el anuncio del último modelo de la empresa intentaba recrear el tono audaz de sus clásicas campañas (mostrando que una leyenda de la NBA de dos metros quince, Wilt Chamberlain, cabía perfectamente en un automóvil compacto), la idea subyacente era muy inferior a la del célebre anuncio «Limón», que utilizó por primera vez la ironía para convertir un Volkswagen en una alternativa aceptable y deseada a las esponjas de gasolina que eran los automóviles norteamericanos.

Durante los años sesenta, la fotografía artística (con frecuencia surrealista) había eclipsado a la ilustración realista como plato fuerte de la publicidad impresa, tendencia que se perpetuó a lo largo de los setenta. No obstante, el público empezaba a estar condicionado por el flujo de imágenes en televisión y demostraba menos interés por las imágenes estáticas. Así, la sutileza y los matices fotográficos propios de la publicidad en prensa de los años cincuenta y sesenta quedaron ensombrecidos por la realidad aplastante de los estudios. La bella mujer afroamericana cuya imagen se utilizó para vender cigarrillos Kent® (p. 35) miraba de manera pasiva pero inequívoca al lector. Y

pese a que este anuncio fue rompedor por utilizar a una modelo negra, el estilo «Te deseo» se hacía palpable como medio estándar de complementar al persuasor bombardeo televisivo. Por descontado, también hubo excepciones a las fotografías típicas. En uno de los anuncios más arrebatadores, el de Time Inc.: «Mientras la imagen estática conmueva... seguiremos en la brecha», una fotografía sensacional de las tropas estadounidenses transportando a un soldado herido fuera del campo de batalla muestra el poder de las instantáneas. Mas, pese a la innegable calidad de este anuncio, muy pocos ejemplos impresos más resultaron tan eficaces.

La ilustración volvió a ponerse ligeramente de moda en la década de los setenta, aunque el resultado solía ser más estilizado y decorativo que intelectual y conceptual. La ilustración del anuncio de Clairol® que presentaba su primera incursión en los champús de esencias vegetales hacía un uso adecuado de un estilo desenfadado y fantasioso, si bien no desafiaba la percepción del público tal y como lo había hecho el clásico Miss Clairol («¿Utiliza... o no?») en 1959. Eso no quiere decir que toda la publicidad comercial debería de ser radical y revolucionaria, ya que, a fin de cuentas, lo importante es atraer la atención del espectador y el objetivo de transmitir un mensaje positivo pesa más que cualquier otro fin. Con todo, en los años setenta se apostó más por las opciones seguras y de eficacia demostrada que por la novedad y los retos.

Los estudiosos de la publicidad señalan que en la década de los setenta reinó la adherencia incondicional y baldía a las pruebas de mercado y a los *targets* de público. La publicidad y la aparición de marcas se estaban convirtiendo en algo demasiado arriesgado y competitivo como para dejar su curso al azar. Para poder determinar la eficacia de la publicidad en televisión y prensa, las agencias se marcaban un público objetivo, que, con frecuencia, podía alterar (o mutilar) campañas para adecuarlas a la opinión general. Mientras que ciertas firmas, como DDB; Ammirati Puris; Foote, Cone & Belding;

Lord, Geller, Federico, Einstein; y George Lois, retuvieron la suficiente influencia creativa para imponerse a los dictámenes del mercado, otras agencias menos establecidas y de corte más general se sometieron a los deseos de los expertos en técnicas de público objetivo. Y no resulta difícil distinguir sus frutos. Los anuncios que condensaban demasiado en una página, como «Las hermanas son diferentes de los hermanos», de productos para el cabello dirigidos a afroamericanos, eran sin duda el resultado de demasiadas sesiones con público objetivo.

Por otro lado, los años setenta fueron testigo del surgimiento de una nueva publicidad. En esa época se empezaron a anunciar líneas de productos naturales, champús y alimentos inclusive, a escala nacional. Las barreras raciales y étnicas caían rápidamente. Se dirigían campañas «étnicas» diferentes a grupos distintos y los afroamericanos y otras «minorías» participaban cada vez más en la publicidad general. Además, se registró un nuevo hito: en la década de los setenta se prohibió la publicidad de tabaco en televisión y se relegó exclusivamente a la prensa, de donde se suprimió también en los años noventa.

El objetivo de la publicidad es ayudar a los clientes a obtener beneficios. La publicidad nunca se ha concebido como un motor cultural, por lo que no tiene sentido esperar que el conjunto de anuncios de cualquier período trascienda su función básica. En cambio, en algunos momentos de la historia, debido a la fuerza creativa de personas con una sensibilidad artística excepcional, la publicidad ha definido la cultura tanto como la música, el cine y la literatura. A menudo, además, ha incorporado y difundido ciertos elementos de esas otras disciplinas. Incluso los aspectos más progresistas de la publicidad se construyen sobre otros fundamentos culturales. Por ejemplo, los publicistas únicamente utilizan las vanguardias cuando ya se han popularizado. Así, la labor de un creativo publicitario con vista consiste en determinar cuándo agitar la marea de un fenómeno único antes de que se coloque en la cresta de la ola. El creativo debe, asi-

mismo, saber qué medio resultará más adecuado para canalizar dicha sacudida.

Para sobrevivir en un mercado competitivo, las revistas se dirigieron a un público cada vez más restringido, lo cual resultaba atractivo para los anunciantes. Mientras que las grandes marcas continuaron aplicando las fórmulas tradicionales de la publicidad y crearon campañas para la televisión, la nueva estrategia de la especialización hizo necesario un replanteamiento global. Incluso en la publicidad impresa, los clientes demandaban una mayor vitalidad para aumentar sus fortunas. Y pese a que aquí se lamente la escasez de creatividad, lo cierto es que en la década de los setenta la publicidad impresa se propuso recuperar parte de sus pérdidas restringiendo su aparición a espacios más reducidos. Eso contribuyó a la aparición de enfoques más ambiciosos e imaginativos en los años ochenta y noventa, épocas en las que, por cierto, las regulaciones y los tabúes referentes al contenido en publicidad volvieron a someterse a examen una vez más.

Steven Heller es director de arte del suplemento «Book Review» del *New York Times* y codirector del programa de máster en Bellas Artes y Diseño de la School of Visual Arts. Es también autor y editor de más de ochenta libros sobre diseño gráfico y cultura popular, entre los que se cuentan: *The Graphic Design Reader, Paul Rand, From Merz to Emigre and Beyond: Avant-Garde Magazine Design of the 20th Century* y *Citizen Design: Perspectives on Design Responsibility*.

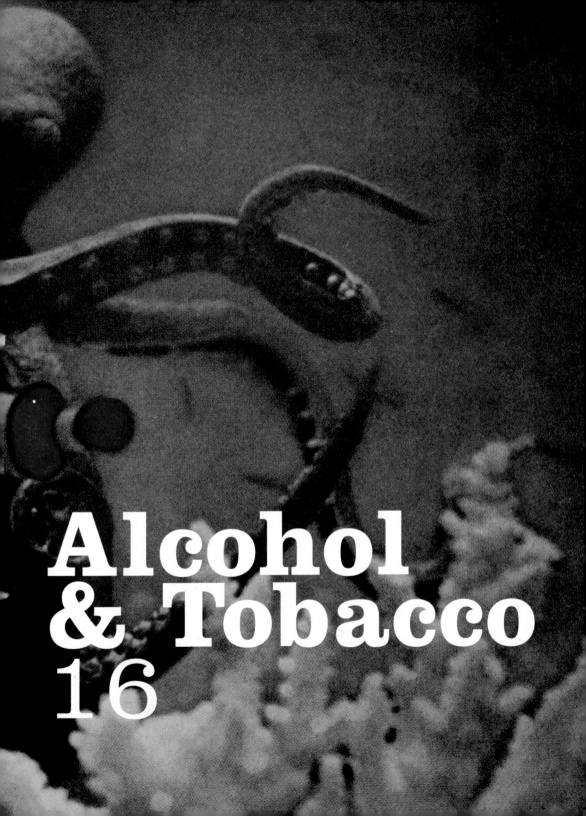

Alcohol
& Tobacco
16

Great Kings of Africa

No. 4 of a series created by noted black artists especially for the brewers of Budweiser. For reprints write: Great Kings No. 4-E, Anheuser-Busch, Inc., St. Louis, Mo. 63118.

Shaka—King of the Zulus (1818–1828)
A strong leader and military innovator, Shaka is noted for revolutionizing 19th century Bantu warfare.

He was first to group regiments by age, and to train his men to use standardized weapons and special tactics. He developed the "assegai," a short stabbing spear, and launched his regiments in tight formation, using large shields to fend off the enemies' throwing spears. Over the years, Shaka's troops earned such a reputation that many enemies would flee at the sight of them.

With cunning and confidence as his tools, Shaka built a small Zulu tribe into a powerful nation of more than one million people, and united all tribes in South Africa against Colonial rule.

The King of Beers,
for a Hundred Years

Budweiser Beer, 1976

Here comes
the **King**
of **Beers!**

Pulling for America for 100 years

Budweiser
1876-1976

The Club Premixed Cocktails, 1975 ◄ *Budweiser Beer, 1976*   ► *Budweiser Beer, 1976* ►► *Almadén Wines, 1977*

BUDWEISER.

presents

JOHN WAYNE

Duke does his first TV special for the King of Beers.... and that is special!

Ice up some Bud® and watch "Swing Out Sweet Land." It's an entertaining, easygoing, 90-minute look on the bright side of America.

★ ALL-STAR CAST ★

(Listed alphabetically)

ANN-MARGRET	MICHAEL LANDON
LUCILLE BALL	DEAN MARTIN
JACK BENNY	ROSS MARTIN
DAN BLOCKER	ED McMAHON
ROSCOE LEE BROWNE	GREG MORRIS
GEORGE BURNS	DAVID NELSON
JOHNNY CASH	RICKY NELSON
ROY CLARK	HUGH O'BRIAN
BING CROSBY	ROWAN & MARTIN
PHYLLIS DILLER	WILLIAM SHATNER
DOODLETOWN PIPERS	RED SKELTON
LORNE GREENE	TOMMY SMOTHERS
CELESTE HOLM	LISA TODD
BOB HOPE	LESLIE UGGAMS
DOUG KERSHAW	DENNIS WEAVER

Sunday, Nov. 29
8:30-10 P.M. EST
NBC-TV

(Check for local time and station)

ANHEUSER-BUSCH, INC. • ST. LOUIS

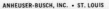

Grapes, like children, mature at different times.

Some we gather at an early age, while the glow of summer is still on the
vine. With others we sit patiently by 'til the hues of autumn manifest themselves.
A sensitive and painstaking art, this parenting of grapes.
Yet well worth our labor of love to produce a wine the calibre
of our Johannisberg Riesling.
Careful harvesting has yielded a Riesling of remarkable
bouquet and truly distinguished class.
Yes, we are very proud parents.

Almadén

THE FRENCH MARTINI.

A couple of drops of cognac on top,
and the perfect martini gin,
Seagram's Extra Dry.

Seagram's Extra Dry.
The Perfect Martini Gin.

"Know why Wolfschmidt Vodka's making such a splash?
    Because it's the only vodka that's won 33 medals!"

"When I hear that, I feel like yelling Bloody Mary!"

Frankfort Distillers Co. New York N.Y.   Made from grain, 80 and 100 proof. Product of U.S.A.

Wolfschmidt.

The genuine vodka with all the medals.

Seagram's Gin, 1974 ◄   Wolfschmidt Vodka, 1971   ► Ronrico Rum, 1970

Ron Rico. Didn't he pioneer the topless bathing suit?

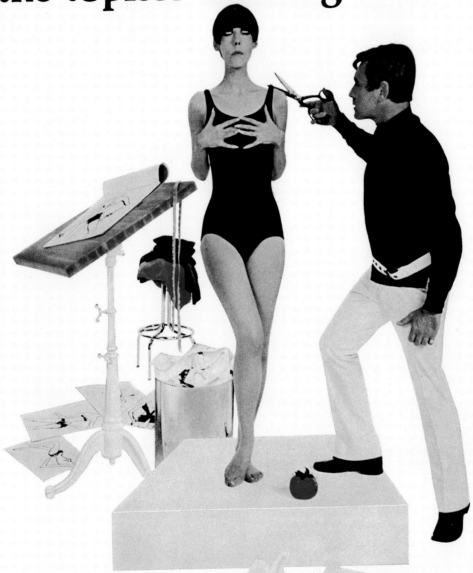

Take it from the top.
Ronrico's a rum. Altogether smooth,
light and very versatile. Untopped
at parties for 112 years. Anyone with eyes knows.

Ronrico. A rum to remember.

OLMECA.
THE HEAD TEQUILA.

In the tradition of the ancient Olmecs

KAHLÚA® & Coffee. Oooh.

Send for our free Kahlúa recipe book. Maidstone Wine & Spirits Inc. 116 No. Robertson Blvd., Los Angeles, CA 90048. Kahlúa Coffee Liqueur from Sunny Mexico. 53 Proof.

Olmeca Tequila, 1977 ◄

Kahlúa Liqueur, 1979

Seagram's V.O.
For people who squeeze all they can out of life.

They seem to do everything. And they do it right. Even when
it comes to having a drink. It has to be Seagram's V.O. Very special.
Very Canadian. Very right. Known by the company it keeps.

Seagram's V̄O Canadian

Orson Welles is the father. And an acclaimed actor.

Rebecca Welles Moede is the daughter. And an aspiring actress.

They're of different generations, these two. But they're very much alike when it comes to the feeling they have for their craft. On this they agree. They live for it. And work for it. And love it.

The Beams, too, have a craft. Different but no less compelling. The Beams' craft is distilling Bourbon. And for six generations now, son has followed father in that craft. Living for it. Working for it. Loving it.

Six generations. One family. One formula. One purpose—the world's finest Bourbon.

It's a proud record.

It's a proud Bourbon—smooth and light and mellow. With a rich aroma full of promise.

Jim Beam. The Bourbon that's been pleasing audiences for 176 (176!) years.

Generation gap? Jim Beam never heard of it.

Jim Beam Bourbon, 1971

What makes her the singer's singer makes us the Scotch drinker's Scotch.

**Black & White.
The Scotch drinker's Scotch.**

Seagram's V.O. Whisky, 1971 ◄

Black & White Scotch, 1972

YUL BRYNNER

Enjoy two great performers

LAUDER'S SCOTCH

Lauder's is the fine Scotch that doesn't cost like a fine Scotch.

Lauder's lets any host turn in a great performance.

86 PROOF

Authentic Scotch Dollar (Crown) minted between 1603-1625. Symbol of Lauder's value.

Yul Brynner stars in "The Ultimate Warrior" from Warner Bros.

Lauder's Scotch, 1975

Design by Bill Blass for Maurice Rentner

The nation's favorite vermouth...sweet or extra dry.

Scotch and the single girl.

Martini & Rossi Vermouth, 1970 ◄ *J&B Scotch, 1971*   ► *Heublein Cocktails, 1979* ► ► *Galaxy Whiskey, 1972*

What paradise tastes lik

Ahh...Exotic Cocktails. Tropical temptations. The essence of wild cherries. Zingy apricots. Juicy guavas. Nature's flavors. Already mixed with brandy. Gin. And secret blends of rum. This is what paradise really tastes like.

A Singapore Sling. A Zombie. Dr. Funk. And Navy Grog. All tropical dreams blended to send shivers through your taste buds. They're marked with mystery and postmarked paradise. So prepare yourself. Few experiences will be as exotic.

Exotic Cocktails. New from Heublein

The age of Galaxy is here.

Discover a whole new world of pure whiskey enjoyment. Mellow-aged. In the timeless tradition of the world's great whiskies. Yet light years ahead in taste and character.

You're probably thinking: *"I've heard whiskey promises before. Can Galaxy really be better than what I'm drinking now?"*

Could be. But then, you'll never know until you put it to your taste, will you?

Look for Galaxy . . . it's out there.

TASTE THE MELLOW GLOW OF TIME IN GALAXY WHISKEY.

DARE YOU BE DIFFERENT

No villain can match the youthful Kabuki character with his great sword and chilling cry — Shibaraku! One of the eighteen favorite Kabuki plays, Shibaraku never fails to please audiences. Another sure crowd pleaser is Suntory Royal Whisky. It's light as a great Scotch, mellow as a distinctive Bourbon, yet different!

For years, incredibly smooth Suntory has been the best selling whisky in Japan. Now, this supreme whisky is a soaring success in the United States. Straight, on-the-rocks, or mixed, serving Suntory is an entertaining idea! Suntory, the classic whisky from Japan.

SUNTORY ROYAL WHISKY

BORN IN ISRAEL

Sabra Liqueur

The essence of the Jaffa orange with just a hint of fine chocolate.

Sabra Liqueur, 1977

The Hiram Walker Sour Ball. For kids over 21.

Didn't you once love the zing of a sour ball? Remember the citrus snap that made you pucker your lips? Remember the cool taste on your tongue?

Now that you've grown up, you're ready to discover the delights of the *Hiram Walker Sour Ball.*

It's a quick treat to mix. (But remember to take it easy. This *Sour Ball's*

(not child's play.)

Just pack your glass with lots of ice, pour in 1½ ounces of Hiram Walker Apricot Flavored Brandy, top it off with the juices of half a lemon and half an orange and stir.

Now relax, and savor that Sour Ball. It's tart to dart, tart to finish.

You'll be surprised how something sour can sweeten up your day.

HIRAM WALKER APRICOT FLAVORED BRANDY

Suntory Royal Whisky, 1971 ◀   *Hiram Walker Brandy, 1978*

A happy DuBouchett to you, too.

27 naturally flavored cordials, all irresistible.

DuBOUCHETT APRICOT TRUE FRUIT FLAVOR Apricot Flavored Brandy

PREPARED AND BOTTLED BY MANY, BLANC & CO. LAWRENCEBURG, IND. & FRESNO, CALIF.

70 PROOF

Just say "Doo-Boo-Shay."

R

DuBouchett Brandy, 1970

33

He's the brains behind the next heavyweight champ.
He'd never smoke a boring cigarette.

Warning: The Surgeon General Has Determined
That Cigarette Smoking Is Dangerous to Your Health.

Viceroy. Where excitement is now a taste.

Enjoy Viceroy flavor–now in a bold new pack.

16 mg. "tar," 1.0 mg. nicotine, av. per cigarette, FTC Report Nov. '75

Viceroy Cigarettes, 1976

▶ *Kent Cigarettes, 1970*

Kent smokes... and that's where it's

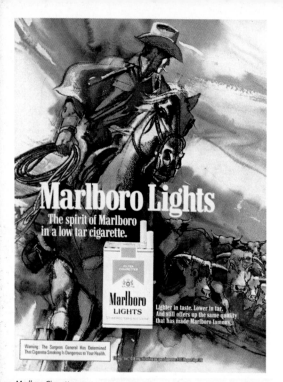

Marlboro Cigarettes, 1977

Marlboro Cigarettes, 1972

Marlboro Cigarettes, 1972

► *Marlboro Cigarettes, 1973*

Come to where
the flavor is

FILTER CIGARETTES

Marlboro

You get a lot to like
with a Marlboro.

America's favorite cigarette break.

Benson & Hedges 100's   *Regular or Menthol*

Benson & Hedges Cigarettes, 1971

Us Tareyton smokers would rather fight than switch!

Tareyton is better / Charcoal is why

Tareyton 100's

Tareyton's activated charcoal delivers a better taste.
A taste no plain white filter can match.

King Size: 19 mg. "tar", 1.3 mg. nicotine; 100 mm: 20 mg. "tar", 1.4 mg. nicotine; av. per cigarette, FTC Report Feb. '73

America's Favorite Cigarette Break.

Benson & Hedges 100's.

In 1913, 1 Mary Patrick got on the train in Boston, got the urge to smoke in New York, 2 decided to light up near Trenton, 3 was caught outside of Wilmington, 4 and was put off the train somewhere between Baltimore and Laurel.

You've come a long way, baby

VIRGINIA SLIMS.

Slimmer than the fat cigarettes men smoke.

Fashions from Beene Bazaar

VIRGINIA SLIMS
MENTHOL·FILTER

VIRGINIA SLIMS
FILTER

Regular: 18 mg. 'tar,' 1.2 mg. nicotine—Menthol: 18 mg. 'tar,' 1.3 mg. nicotine av. per cigarette, FTC Report Apr. '72

This is L&M–super bad

That show was out-of-sight.
You can still feel every note.
They played hot and hard.
They gave you the truth.
And now
you're both ripe for L&M.

Ah, the taste of an L&M menthol cigarette–super bad.

Warning: The Surgeon General Has Determined That Cigarette Smoking Is Dangerous to Your Health.

L&M Menthol,
19 mg. "tar," 1.2 mg. nicotine
av. per cigarette by FTC method.

Virgina Slims Cigarettes, 1972 ◄

L&M Cigarettes, 1971

45

Auto–
mobiles
46

$3,986.65.*

FOR 1970: A NEW FLIGHT OF BIRDS

Soaring into the '70's far ahead of the rest...
1970 Thunderbird. With dramatic new front-
end styling, shaped to slice the wind.
Longer, lower and wider for '70. Yet, still uniquely
Thunderbird. With its impressive list of standard
luxury features you'd pay extra for in other
cars. Options other cars don't even offer. And
standards of quality most others only aspire to.
Choose from three distinctive models.
The New Flight of Birds is ready for take-off.

Above: Pan Am's® Boeing 747 Jet and the 1970 Thunderbird
2-Door Landau with Special Brougham interior.

THUNDERBIRD

Ford Thunderbird, 1973

Ford Thunderbird, 1970 ◀

Mercury, 1971

"Forward Motion"

New Datsun 1200 Sport Coupe.
An original portrait by Peter Max.

The new Datsun 1200 is today's kind of car. It's an economical package of motion and fun that's nice for you...and for the world around you. So when we commissioned its portrait, we went to today's kind of artist—Peter Max—probably the best known artist of his generation, a creative genius who made colorful visions an exciting part of everyday life.

The new Datsun 1200 Sport Coupe gave him a subject that's exciting on several levels. For the ecology minded, it's a car that doesn't cost much money, doesn't take up much space and gets around 30 miles out of every gallon of gasoline. At the same time it has quick handling and spirited performance. Finally, it comes with all the niceties you could want—fully reclining bucket seats, safety front disc brakes, flow-through ventilation—and a few you didn't expect—a fold-down rear seat storage area, whitewalls and tinted glass, for instance. Peter Max has captured the spirit of our 1200, a Datsun Original. Capture it for yourself in real, everyday terms at your Datsun dealer. Drive a Datsun...then decide.

Own a Datsun Original.
From Nissan with Pride

The AMC Gremlin.
More fun than a barrel
of gas bills.

The Gremlin is an economical small car with the room, ride and comfort of a bigger car. It's economical because it has an efficient 4-cylinder engine and 4-speed gear box, which manage to be very thrifty and very peppy at the same time.

The Gremlin also comes with a lot of things that make it more fun to drive. 4 on the floor, wide-track handling and easy maneuverability, give the Gremlin quite a sporty feel. And casual Levi seats, racing stripes and slot style wheels give the Gremlin X quite a sporty look to go with it.

You also get AMC's exclusive BUYER PROTECTION PLAN, with the only full 12 month/12,000 mile warranty. That means AMC will fix, or replace free any part, except tires, for 12 months or 12,000 miles whether the part is defective, or just plain wears out under normal use and service.

Discover how much fun, and how economical, driving can be with a perky, practical Gremlin.

Based on EPA estimated ratings, 35 highway, 22 city, 27 combined for the optional 4-cylinder engine with 4-speed manual transmission. Your actual mileage may vary depending on your car's condition, optional equipment, and how and where you drive. California figures lower.

AMC Gremlin
The fun Americans want.
The size America needs.

® BUYER PROTECTION PLAN is reg. U.S. Pat. and Tm. Off.

Datsun 1200, 1973 ◀ *American Motors Gremlin, 1977*

▶ *Ford Mustang, 1972* ▶▶ *Volvo, 1974*

Control and balance make it a beautiful experience

You don't sail a boat just to get across the water.

The fun is in the doing.

The pleasure of motion under control.

Mustang drivers understand t

If all they wanted was to get fro here to there, they'd be driving something else. Not a Ford Mus

With independent front suspe sion and an anti-sway bar to give you good control, good road handling.

With bucket seats to position comfortably behind the wheel.

With a cockpit design and floc mounted shift that give you a beautiful feeling the instant you inside.

There are five sporty Mustang models: Hardtop, SportsRoof, Convertible, Mach 1, Grandé. And a selection of five engines, three transmissions. What it takes to make driving a beautifu experience is what Ford puts into Mustang.

1972 Mustang Mach 1

FORD MUSTAN

FORD DIVISION

BEAT THE SYSTEM. BUY A VOLVO.

Can you still get prime quality for $1.26 a pound?

A pound of Volkswagen isn't cheap compared to other cars. But what you pay for is the quality. Prime quality.

Just look at what you get for your money:

13 pounds of paint, some of it in places you can't even see. (So you can leave a Volkswagen out overnight and it won't spoil.)

A watertight, airtight, sealed steel bottom that protects against rocks, rain, rust and rot.

Over 1,000 inspections per one Beetle.

1,014 inspectors who are so finicky that they reject parts you could easily ride around with and not even detect there was anything wrong.

Electronic Diagnosis that tells you what's right and wrong with important parts of your car.

A 1600 cc aluminum-magnesium engine that gets 25* miles to a gallon of regular gasoline.

Volkswagen's traditionally high resale value.

Over 22,000 changes and improvements on a car that was well built to begin with.

What with all the care we take in building every single Volkswagen, we'd like to call it a filet mignon of a car. Only one problem. It's too tough.

Few things in life work as well as a Volkswagen.

Action is having an electronic fuel-injected 2.0-liter engine take you from 0 to 60 in 11.0 seconds.

Action is stopping on radial tires with 4-wheel disc brakes.

Action is taking a corner with rack-and-pinion steering in a mid-engine car and feeling closer to the road than the white line.

The

Action is a 5-speed gearbox.

Action is a light, fiberglass roof you can take off in less than a minute.

Action is sporting a built-in roll bar.

Action is 13 of the wildest colors you've ever seen. From Zambezi Green to Signal Orange.

Action

lon and a cruising range of more than 400 miles on one tank of gas.

Action is finally stopping for gas and having all the station attendants wanting to wait on you.

Action is what you get every time you step into a mid-engine Porsche 914.

Porsche

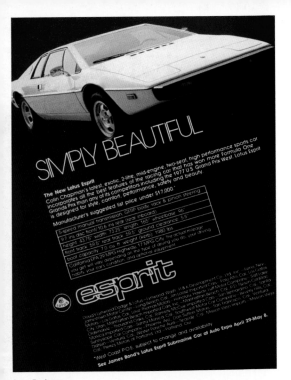

SIMPLY BEAUTIFUL

The New Lotus Esprit
Colin Chapman's latest, exotic, 2-litre, mid-engine, two-seat, high performance sports car incorporates all the best features of the racing car that has won more Formula One Grands Prix than any of its competitors including the 1977 U.S. Grand Prix West. Lotus Esprit is designed for style, comfort, performance, safety and beauty.

Manufacturer's suggested list price under $17,000.

5-speed manual transmission. GFRP body, rack & pinion steering.

97 ins disc front/10.6 ins rear (rear inboard)
97 ins disc front/10.6 ins rear width 73.25 length 165" wheelbase 96
height 43.75 width 73.25 length 165" ground clearance 5.5
front track 59.5 rear track 59.5 ground clearance 5.5
boot capacity 7.0 cu ft weight 1980 lbs
California EPA 29 MPG highway, 17 MPG City. The actual mileage you get will vary depending on the type of driving you do, your driving habits, your car's condition, and optional equipment.

*West Coast P.O.E. subject to change and availability
See James Bond's Lotus Esprit Submarine Car at Auto Expo April 29-May 8.

Dough Lynwood Dodge & Lotus - Lynwood, Wash. J & K Development Co., Ltd., Inc. - Turbo New Somerhaven Motor Center - Long Beach, Cal. Jim Loose Imported Cars - Tustin Alfa Cal - Los Gatos Motor, Utah Montana Motor - Portland, Ore. Monmouth Import - Fort Motor Company - Salt Lake City, Utah, Washington Beach, Importization, Inc. - Washington Beach, Cal. Nissan Carolina, Southland - Thousand - Santa Monica, Inc. Southwest Motor Cal - Santa Monica - Beverly Hills, Cal. Oldsmobile Imported Company - Phoenix, Ariz. Audi Sun Button Motor Cal - Sun Trafford, Cal., Ventura Ranciraola Venturas - Alaska Foreign Auto - Seaside Cal. Mission Viejo Imports - Mission Viejo Datsun Ventura Co. Alaska Foreign Portland, Ore. Cox Press Motor of Portland Ltd. - Portland, Ore

esprit

Lotus Esprit, 1977

"That's IT"

Just as a great painting is more than canvas and paints, there are some things that go beyond the sum of their parts. The Porsche Targa is such an object.

It is a piece of machinery whose purpose far exceeds transporting you from one point to another. The Targa's goal is to afford the ultimate driving experience. In performance, in engineering, in comfort.

The Targa has come amazingly close to that goal; each year, with subtle improvements, a bit more.

First, consider its superbly thought-out features. It has a built-in roll bar, and a huge fixed rear window. To give the car the practicality of a hardtop coupe. And you the exhilarating experience of a roadster.

It has an aerodynamic shape, to protect you from wind blast. And a rear-engine design that has been steadily improved upon for 25 years.

All controls are meticulously engineered to be functional and logically accessible.

Yet it is the total effect of these innovations that impresses.

With the removable top stored in the trunk, cushioned in luxurious bucket seats, you ride in "Belle Epoque" comfort.

But the grandest feature of the Targa is the experience of driving it.

The handling is quick, correct, precise, because of Porsche's legendary engineering. Putting the driver and car in perfect collab-oration. It is almost as if you just "think" where you want the car to go.

The Targa is available in all three 911 models: 911T, 911E, and 911S.

But be warned.

It is very difficult to be humble about owning any Porsche. And if it's a Targa, that's IT.

Volvo, 1971 ◄ ◄ ◄ *Volkswagen, 1973* ◄ ◄ *Porsche 914, 1973* ◄

Porsche Targa, 1973

There's a Firebird for every purpose.
Except standing still.

Esprit offers luxury that doesn't get in the way of sport. Individually-cushioned buckets of supple vinyl. A rosewood-vinyl accented dash. Plush cut-pile carpet underfoot. Plus an available "Sky Bird" Package with sky blue paint, matching wheels and special trim throughout.
 Formula Firebird is for people who are driven by a love of driving. Who are forever inspired by dual

simulated air scoops atop a 5.0 litre V-8. Who can appreciate stabilizer bars and steel-belted radials.
 Trans Am is the ultimate Firebird. Built to go all the way. An eye-catching, head-turning, heart-wrenching, awe-inspiring legend.
 A lot of it has to do with the ominous air extractors, deflectors and air dam. The shrieking bird available for the hood. And the

6.6 litre V-8 underneath.
 Even the base Firebird has a purpose. To deliver Firebird's fire at an appealing price.
 Firebirds are equipped with GM-built engines produced by various divisions. Your dealer has details. He also has a Firebird for whatever you like to do.
 Unless you like standing still.
 Pontiac ▼ The Mark of Great Cars

1978 ▼ Pontiac's best year yet!

Pontiac Firebird, 1978

▶ *Cadillac, 1975*

Determination has its rewards.

tradition of building great cars like the 1933 Cadillac 355 Phaeton has its advantages—and
wards—for today's luxury car buyer. First, we stubbornly maintain that a luxury car should
e a thing of beauty. This is reflected in all nine Cadillacs—including Eldorado, the only
merican-built luxury convertible. Then, there's Total Cadillac Value. Because of it, Cadillac
sale is traditionally the highest of any U.S. luxury car make...and its repeat ownership
e greatest of any U.S. car make. Cadillac. **Then and Now...an American Standard for the World.**

Cadillac '75

MG Midget.
High-flying fun.
Low-flying pricetag.

In the wide-open MG Midget, you can fly now, pay little, and even save money on gas while enjoying all the fun of owning a real, live, top-down sports car while you're still young enough to enjoy it.

The Midget is, in fact, the lowest-priced true sports car on the market.

The Midget has rack and pinion steering, short-throw four-speed stick, front disc brakes and an agility in turns and a feel for the road that make it a joy to handle. Not to mention an impressive EPA-rated 34 MPG on the highway and 22 MPG in the city. (Naturally, these are estimates and the actual mileage you get may vary depending on the car's condition and how and where you drive, optional equipment, and may be lower in California.)

If whatever you're driving is getting you down, go fly a Midget. It's fun. It's inexpensive. It's thrifty to run. For the name of the dealer nearest you, call these numbers toll-free: (800) 447-4700, or, in Illinois, (800) 322-4400.

British Leyland Motors Inc., Leonia, New Jersey 07605.

MG Midget, 1977

▶ *Porsche 924, 1979*

LEASE A LEGEND. THE PORSCHE 924.

Why lease an ordinary car when you can lease a new 1979 Porsche?

The Porsche 924.

It's designed to carry on the Porsche tradition of winning. A tradition that spans 31 years and includes over 400 major racing victories.

It's also designed for the practicality of today. Its unique rear transaxle provides virtually perfect 50-50 weight distribution between front and rear—for balanced road holding and braking.

Its aerodynamic design is aesthetically pleasing—and practical. In wind tunnel tests, it registers an amazingly low drag co-efficient of only 0.36.

Best of all, even with options, leasing a 924 is surprisingly affordable.

So visit your Porsche + Audi dealer and test drive a living legend.

PORSCHE + AUDI
NOTHING EVEN COMES CLOSE

Introducing the Jeep CJ/5 in "Jeans"

Look what the well dressed Jeep CJ/5 is wearing! New Levi's® styled seats with matching fold-down top. Made of rugged, easy to care for vinyl fabric in absolutely authentic styling—right down to the copper rivets. Built to take plenty of rough treatment and most anything the weather can dish out.

Choose Levi's® blue or Levi's® tan—to complement vehicle color.

The Levi's® interior is standard on the Jeep Renegade (shown above) and optional on the standard Jeep CJ/5.

Levi's® and Jeep Corporation—two names at home in the great outdoors—waiting for you! Jeep wrote the book on 4-wheel drive.

Jeep ▚ CJ/5

From a Subsidiary of
American Motors Corporation

Jeep CJ/5, 1974

This is Cordoba. The small Chrysler. An automobile in which you will enjoy not only great comfort . . . but great confidence. It is confidence you can see, the confidence of knowing your automobile possesses a look of great dignity. It is confidence you can *feel*, in thickly cushioned contour-seats available in rich crushed velour or soft Corinthian leather. It is confidence you experience when you are in control of a truly road worthy automobile. This is the confidence you will find in a most surprisingly affordable small Chrysler, Cordoba.

Chrysler Cordoba, 1975

▶ *Plymouth Sapporo, 1978*

Standard dual pow
assisted sport mirr

Concealed adjustable headrests.

Standard sport v

Standard inside deck release.

Standard adjustable
lumbar supports

ushion

PRESS

Standard tachometer, oil and amp gauges
and trip odometer.

Standard tilt steering column.

Standard forced air
ventilation.

Optional
air conditioning.

Optional AM-FM rad
with cassette.

Standard 5-speed transmission
(Automatic shown, optional).

Optional power windows.

Le City Car

One of the reasons Le Car has caused so much excitement in this country is because of what it can do in the city. There isn't a car in town that can match Le Car for parking, maneuverability, ease of handling and smooth ride.

Le Car fits in a smaller parking space than any other car in its class.

Even though Le Car has a longer wheelbase than Honda Civic or VW Rabbit, it has a shorter overall length. So Le Car will fit in a space

that the others have to pass by. Add to this Le Car's short 32-foot turning circle and you can see why the parking problems of the city are no problem for Le Car.

A highly responsive car that handles with ease.

Parking is not the only difficulty you'll encounter in the city. Driving is another. Le Car is equipped with front-wheel drive, rack and pinion steering, four-wheel independent suspension and Michelin steel-belted radials, all standard. (Honda, Rabbit, Chevette and Fiesta don't offer this combination of standard features.) The result is that Le Car can zip in and out of, around and through traffic.

And Le Car's ride is so remarkably smooth that Car & Driver reported, "The rough-road ride in Le Car is a new standard for small cars. It waltzed across the worst roads we could find—the cratered surfaces of Manhattan—as though it was fresh pavement."

Although Le Car is small on the

outside you could never tell from its roomy inside. Le Car is designed to give you the most interior room while using the least exterior space.

A world of satisfied Le Car owners.

In Europe, nearly two million people drive Le Car with a passion. That's more than Fiesta and Rabbit combined. Here in America, Le Car sales more than doubled in 1977. What's more, in an independent study, Le Car owner satisfaction was rated an amazingly high 95%. The price for all this? A very satisfying $3495.*

Obviously, a lot of people are doing a lot more than just driving Le Car in the city. So if you really want to see how much fun Le Car can be, flip open the giant sun roof (optional) and take Le City Car for a drive in the country. For more information call 800-631-1616 for your nearest dealer. In New Jersey call collect 201-461-6000.

*P.O.E. East Coast: Price excludes transportation, dealer preparation and taxes. Stripe, Mag wheels, Sun roof and Rear wiper/washer optional at extra cost. Prices higher in the West. Renault USA, Inc. ©1978.

Le Car by Renault ◊

Renault Le Car, 1978

▶ Volkswagen Rabbit, 1979

GOOD NEWS FOR PEOPLE 7'2" AND UNDER.

If you've always thought a little car meant a lot of crowding, you've obviously never looked into a Volkswagen Rabbit.

There happens to be so much room in a Rabbit that all 7'2" of Wilt Chamberlain can fit comfortably into the driver's seat.

With space left over.

Because the Rabbit has even more headroom than a Rolls-Royce.

As well as more room for people and things than practically every other imported car in its class.

Including every Datsun. Every Toyota. Every Honda, Mazda, and Renault.

Not to mention every small Ford and Chevy.

And, of course, what's all the more impressive about the room you get in a Rabbit is that it comes surrounded by the Rabbit itself. The car that, according to Car and Driver Magazine, "...does more useful and rewarding things than any other small car in the world..."

So how can you go wrong?

With the Rabbit you not only get the comfort of driving the most copied car in America.

You also get the comfort of driving a very comfortable car.

Because it may look like a Rabbit on the outside.

But it's a Rabbit on the inside.

VOLKSWAGEN DOES IT AGAIN

Ford Cruising Van, 1977

Harley-Davidson, 1977

▶ *Cragar Custom Wheels, 1978*

ON THE STREET.

Bright chrome is in. So is Cragar with a trio that really shines. The popular spoked S/S has always been the custom wheel king. Now, it has a pair of regal companions in the solid SS/T and Slick Dish with Wire Basket. A royal selection of applications and sizes in all three. Cragar does it—on the street.

Easy Rider

When the easy rider left the highways and took to the trails, the riding wasn't so easy any more. Then came the Arctic Cat Bikes.

With the easy ride of shock absorber suspension at both ends.

With the easy ride engineered by Arctic Cat's back trail experts.

With the shiftless luxury of automatic transmission.

So now the easy rider is still off the highways, and he's riding easy again.

Quickly, quietly and dependably, too. Choose one of four models and start riding easy with Arctic Cat Bikes.

Arctic Cat Bikes
Get away from it all. And all the way back.

Arctic Cat Bikes, 1971

▸ Appliance Industries Wheels, 1972

Look for Appliance.

our years in the making, here's **WIRE MAG**™ the revolutionary new wheel from Appliance. Our own one piece, high strength alloy design*, with mirror polished finish. **WIRE MAG** is available in all popular sizes, easy to install, guaranteed tubeless and of course, fits disc brakes. **WIRE MAG** is the latest in a wide range of custom wheels from Appliance. Every one — whether Chrome, Spoke Mag, Dish Mag or the all new **WIRE MAG** is built to the same highest standards of style and quality, at a price you can afford. Ask your dealer, he knows. Look for Appliance, you'll like what you see.

Patent Pending

APPLIANCE INDUSTRIES
23920 South Vermont Avenue, Harbor City, California 90710

Electra Glide.
On the road it stands alone.

1200cc Electra Glide. Big-twin performance that keeps you hanging in on any tour. Dependable power and comfort on the open highway or heavy country. Cast and polished covers. Trouble-free Bendix carburetor for quick, all weather starts, smooth throttle response. High-output alternator, push-button starter. Timeless elegance of the world's finest motorcycle. Electra Glide. Road riders' choice. From Harley-Davidson. Number one where it counts . . . on the road and in the records. AMF | HARLEY-DAVIDSON, Milwaukee, Wisconsin 53201.

the Harley-Davidson outperformer

1977 GuzziMatic

It's here! Moto Guzzi's 1977 revolutionary, 1000cc Automatic. An unparalleled blend of design and engineering in a truly unique machine.

An automatic, torque converter transmission which eliminates the chore of constant shifting. A new, emergency sidestand that automatically locks the rear wheel to prevent unexpected rolling. Electronic petcocks meter the flow of fuel through the twin carbs. Special air spoilers on the front safety bars increase high speed stability. Air and oil filters increase performance and engine life. Standard footboards and high handle bars provide added touring comfort.

And when you're ready to ease the Guzzimatic to a stop, an exclusive patented triple-disc integral braking system provides safe, sure stopping power.

All this plus Guzzi's race-tested cradle frame and suspension molded around a smooth, reliable shaft drive and a host of other owner benefits give the Guzzimatic a new mark in motorcycling individuality.

Inspect the exceptional, 1977 Guzzimatic 1000 at your nearest Guzzi dealer soon and see for yourself why Guzzi has become the increasing choice of knowledgeable motorcyclists. Available this year in four distinctive colors, black, silver, white and silver blue.

The Machine Built Exclusively For Unlimited Touring . . . In Style.

PREMIER
MOTOR CORP.
Hasbrouck Heights, New Jersey 07604
Exclusive Distributer in U.S. & Canada

Matching saddlebags standard equipment. Windshield optional.

CIRCLE NO. 21 ON READER SERVICE PAGE.

GuzziMatic Motorcycle, 1977

showroom showdown

$1998.

CB-750K The brand-new 1977 Honda CB-750K is a great machine. The eighth-generation son of the first of the modern-day superbikes. An overhead cam, four-cylinde, four-stroke engine powers this stylish, proven performer. And now it's being listed at the manufacturer's suggested retail price of only $1,998? That's right, $1,998. Hundreds of dollars less than you might expect. And that $1,998 price is not a specially-reduced sale price. That's the everyday price which this year includes an set-up charges. This year the 750K has received some really neat performance and comfort changes. Like carburetors equipped with an accelerator pump for snappier throttle response, a new free-gallon tank, four seamless mufflers, one contoured seat and new handlebars with soft neoprene grips. There are responsive, free-valve-type hydraulic front forks, a new 17-inch rear rim and 4.50 cross-section tire for better ride. Plus the one feature that comes standard on every Honda motorcycle—proven Honda reliability. At only $1,998 it's a great way to go. The new 1977 CB-750K has never been better, nor has the time to buy one.

going strong in the showroom!
HONDA

Honda Motorcycle, 1977

Some bikes challenge egos.

You don't just jump on a Bonnie and take off. The Bonneville is a motorcycle that demands involvement. A vertical twin that insists you learn exactly how to tickle the carbs . . . throttle just right . . . so one healthy kick brings it roaring to life. Bonneville riders—over two generations of them—understand and appreciate this intimate bond between man and machine. Most egos aren't up to the kind of a trip that today's 750cc Bonnie demands. But if yours is, we have a most rewarding motorcycle for you.

1201 State College Parkway, Anaheim, California 92806 **The Bonneville for '77.**
CIRCLE NO. 22 ON READER SERVICE PAGE.

Harley-Davidson, 1971 ◄   *Bonneville Motorcycle, 1977*

INTRODUCING A WOLF IN WOLF'S CLOTHING.

It comes dressed in special paint, a sleek teardrop tank, flashy megaphone pipes, and lots of chrome. All the markings of a bigger beast.

And like its big brothers, it's ridden in a more natural, laid-back position. With a low-riding stepped seat. And handlebars that reach back for you instead of the other way around.

But our XS400 has more than the profile. It has the power.

In fact, *Cycle Guide* magazine found that it's the fastest accelerating four-stroke 400 you can buy. And one of the best handling motorcycles anywhere.

Or, as they put it, "the only limit to how much fun you have is how much lean angle you like."

How did all this come about? Engineering.

For example, the suspension system not only gives you big bike steadiness, but it can be fine tuned for any rider, any riding style.

And the carburetors automatically adjust to engine load. So there's a lot of power, but not a lot of temperament.

Plus there are features like an overhead cam, electric starting, 6-speed transmission, self-cancelling turn signals, disc brakes, and

complete instrumentation that's angled back for easier reading.

There's even an economy model, the XS400-2F, for those of you on a little tighter budget. It has wire wheels instead of cast alloy, slightly less chrome, a kick starter, drum brakes. And it comes in one color instead of two. In all other respects, it's identical to our regular model.

Which means it does a whole lot more than look like a bigger bike.

It acts like one.

YAMAHA
When you know how they're built.

Yamaha Motorcycle, 1979

THE '78 FORD BRONCO.

COMPARE IT TO ANY 4-WHEELER, ANYWHERE.

The first 4-wheeler that puts it all together.
Introducing Ford's all-new Bronco with... 1. Big cube 5.8L (351) V-8 standard... 2. Choice of part-time 4 WD with optional automatic... 3. Rear foot-well for seating comfort... 4. Rear flip-fold seat option for usable cargo space... 5. Four-speed transmission... 6. Front quad shock option... 7. Free Wheeling package option... 8. Off-road handling package option... 9. Privacy™ Glass option... 10. Choice of bucket or optional front bench seats... 11. Front stabilizer bar. Bronco: Winner of the Four Wheeler Of The Year award from Four Wheeler magazine, October 1977.

Front quad shock option

Choice of part-time 4WD

Rear flip-fold seat option

FORD
FORD DIVISION

Ford Bronco, 1978

New Ford Ranchero... Right on!

AM/FM Stereo Radio—with space-age microcircuitry, surrounds you in faithful stereo sound.

Performance Cluster—includes tachometer, odometer, clock, ammeter, water temperature and oil pressure gauges.

Hood Scoop Standard on GT Model—functional with Ram-Air induction on 351 (4V) and 429 V-8 engines.

High-back Bucket Seats—for individual comfort; high-back bench seat is standard.

Four-on-the-floor—fully synchronized 4-speed transmission with quick-shift Hurst® mechanism.

Super Wide G-70s—really grab the road when you want to hang in there.

Deluxe Three-spoke Steering Wheel. Rim-blow feature gives fingertip horn control.

Magnum 500 Chrome Wheels—the ultimate in "mag" type wheels. Available on all models.

No question of who you are in a Ranchero, because your Ranchero can be a one-of-a-kind pickup, designed by you from a string of with-it options you wouldn't believe. Some are shown above. And

Ranchero's all new for '72. New size, new style, new engineering, new satisfaction. And the pickup box is both wider and longer. Visit your Ford Dealer and check the specs. Then roll your own!

A better idea for safety: Buckle up.

FORD RANCHERO

Ford Ranchero, 1972

SCOUT® II BEATS BLAZER. COMING AND GOING.

The 4-wheel drive Scout is trim where it counts, and more maneuverable than a Chevy Blazer. Scout's designed from the ground up to be a better performing off-road machine. It's 9½ inches narrower to get you through those tight spots Blazer can't handle. Five inches lower in overall height. But with the same ground clearance as Blazer.

Scout gives you a better approach angle than Blazer. Scout's 44% approach angle at its lowest point means you're far less likely to dig in and hang up your front end in those tough uphill conditions.

Scout is shorter with a tighter turning circle than Blazer. A full 3 feet 8 inches tighter. That's one heck of a difference when your turning around on a dead-end trail.

Scout carries more payload than Blazer. Scout's built tough to take it. And engineered to carry more. 35% more payload. That's an extra 643 pounds more than Blazer. Hundreds of pounds more gear, passengers, and camping equipment.

Scout has a longer cargo bed than Blazer. With rear seats up, Scout gives you nearly half a foot more cargo bed length than Blazer.

Scout's rear seat folded forward and Blazer's stationary rear seat left bolted in place, Scout gives you 29 inches more usable cargo bed length than Blazer. For a total cargo bed length of almost 5 feet.

Scout conveniently gives you maximum cargo by simply folding up the rear seat. But for maximum cargo length in a Blazer, you have to unbolt and leave your rear seat behind.

Find out for yourself what rugged design is all about. Test drive the incredible Scout II at your International Harvester dealer today.

Yes, I'm interested in more detailed information on Scout's design specs and off-road features. Please send me the brochures I've checked below. Enclosed is 50¢ for postage and handling.   706LBAM

☐ Scout® II
☐ Scout Traveler®
☐ Scout Terra™ Pickup
☐ Scout® Diesels
☐ Scout® Towing/RV Applications

Name _____
        Please print
Phone _____
Address _____
City _____ State ___ Zip ___

Mail to: Scout Brochure
International Harvester
P.O. Box 1909, Mossville, IL 61552

SCOUT THE AMERICA OTHERS PASS BY.

INTERNATIONAL HARVESTER

International Harvester Scout, 1977

Introducing Ranchero/77.

For the man in charge.

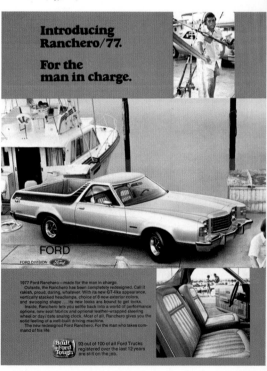

FORD
FORD DIVISION

1977 Ford Ranchero—made for the man in charge.
Outside, the Ranchero has been completely redesigned. Call it rakish, proud, daring, whatever. With its new GT-like appearance, vertically stacked headlamps, choice of 6 new exterior colors, and swooping shape ..., the new looks are bound to get looks.
Inside, Ranchero lets you settle back into a world of performance options, new seat fabrics and optional leather-wrapped steering wheel or day/date analog clock. Most of all, Ranchero gives you the solid feeling of a well-built driving machine.
The new redesigned Ford Ranchero. For the man who takes command of his life.

Built Ford Tough
93 out of 100 of all Ford Trucks registered over the last 12 years are still on the job.

Ford Ranchero, 1977   ▶ *Ford Ranchero, 1972*

ew Ford Ranchero...the pickup car!

If you've an idea Ford's all-new Ranchero is a high-spirited sports car, you're right. If you think Ranchero is a handy, hard-working pickup, right again. For Ranchero is a beautiful blending of both. It offers a ride that's both smoother and quieter with a wheelbase that's four inches longer than last year. New strength and durability with a solid big-car frame. And clean responsive handling with a new link coil rear suspension. Front disc brakes are standard, and you can choose any of six spirited engines up to a 429 V8. Big new loadspace, too, with a new box that's longer at the rail and wider at the floor. 4-foot panels easily slide between wheelhousings. And campers or boaters will welcome a new towing capacity of up to 6,000 pounds. See a Ranchero 500, GT or Squire at your Ford Dealer's soon. With so much that's so right, you can't go wrong.

A better idea for safety: Buckle up.

All-new FORD RANCHERO

Bob Hope says,
"Cancel My Reservation, I'll take my Apollo."

Bob Hope, star of Naho Enterprises Productions' "Cancel My Reservation," from Warner Bros., always uses his Apollo Motor Home for motion picture locations, mobile office, golf vacations, and cruising enjoyment. Bob says, "Apollo is the only way to go for safety and luxurious accommodations — it gives me all that privacy and Ring-Of-Steel construction."
You need no reservation to see your Apollo dealer for a new experience in first class living on-the-go. He will be delighted to show you Apollo's exciting, new 1973 line of 22, 25, and 30 foot models in a variety of floor plans and beautiful decorator-coordinated interiors. Features include a bath with sunken tub/shower, sparkling kitchen, and livingroom comfort all contained in a weatherproof, reinforced fiberglass body. Like Bob Hope, drive your Apollo today. For complete information and dealer nearest you, write Apollo Motor Homes, Inc., 9250 Washburn Road, Downey, Calif. 90242.

Select Dealerships available

RING OF STEEL CONSTRUCTION   MEANS RING OF SAFETY

APOLLO
MOTOR HOMES
a subsidiary of Kalvex Inc.

Watch Bob Hope Specials on NBC-TV

"Women only drive automatic transmissions."

Some car manufacturers actually believe women buy cars for different reasons than men do.

So they build "a woman's car." Oversized, hopelessly automatic and dull.

At Honda we designed just one thing. A lean, spunky economy car with so much pizzazz it handles like a sports car.

If you're bored with cars designed only to get you from point A to point B, without responding to you the driver, maybe you ought to take the Honda Civic for a spin.

We've got a stick shift with an astonishing amount of zip. Enough to surprise you. We promise.

Or, if you prefer, Hondamatic.™ It's a semi-automatic transmission that gives you convenience, but doesn't rob you of involvement.

Neither one is a woman's car.

Honda Civic.
We don't make "a woman's car."

Business
&
Industry
84

Otis
Elevator Company

Our future is a vertical marketplace FEB 7 6

It's a high-rise shopping center with the excitement of an old world bazaar and the convenience of true one-stop shopping. It's also a cultural center with drama, art and music. It's vertical because that's the best way to use our dwindling supply of urban land.

And because Otis has more than 60 years' experience in safely moving people, automatically, we know how to predict traffic patterns, handle load requirements and plan for the vertical and horizontal transportation requirements for such a marketplace.

When it's built, we'll combine conventional elevators and escalators with self-propelled horizontal elevators to speed you from floor-to-floor and shop-to-shop. Even move you quickly by automated transit from urban transportation and parking facilities into the shopping area.

Because we believe in the future growth of the world's cities, Otis research is working now on ideas to better move people and goods tomorrow. **Otis, a company in motion.**

Master Charge Card, 1970 ◄ ◄   *Otis Elevator Co., 1974* ◄   *Otis Elevator Co., 1976*

**How to branch way out
without pulling up your roots**

Cover ground by phone.
Specifically, by a new money-
saving Long Distance service
called WATS—Wide Area
Telecommunications Service.
With WATS, you pay a flat
monthly charge regardless
of the number or length of
your calls. It's not unusual to
get more than twice as much
calling time for your Long
Distance dollars. And you
can buy WATS nationally
or regionally. Ask one
of our Communications
Consultants what WATS
can do for your business.

AT&T

This isn't the generation gap we're worried about.

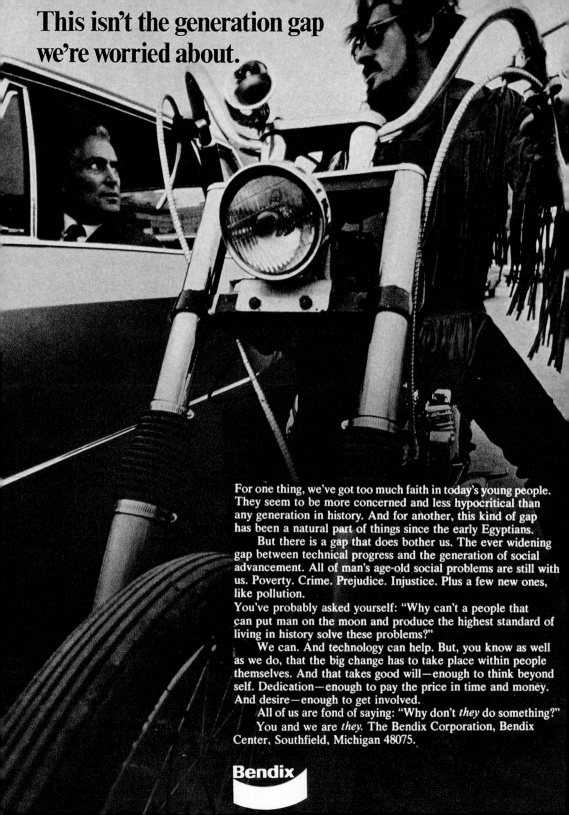

For one thing, we've got too much faith in today's young people. They seem to be more concerned and less hypocritical than any generation in history. And for another, this kind of gap has been a natural part of things since the early Egyptians.

But there is a gap that does bother us. The ever widening gap between technical progress and the generation of social advancement. All of man's age-old social problems are still with us. Poverty. Crime. Prejudice. Injustice. Plus a few new ones, like pollution.

You've probably asked yourself: "Why can't a people that can put man on the moon and produce the highest standard of living in history solve these problems?"

We can. And technology can help. But, you know as well as we do, that the big change has to take place within people themselves. And that takes good will—enough to think beyond self. Dedication—enough to pay the price in time and money. And desire—enough to get involved.

All of us are fond of saying: "Why don't *they* do something?"

You and we are *they*. The Bendix Corporation, Bendix Center, Southfield, Michigan 48075.

Bendix

They're trying to tell us something.

We're foolish not to listen.

The Arab nations have indicated their intention to control oil production in order to keep prices up.

They're just not going to let the world use their limited resource as a cheap fuel.

For them it may be the right thing to do. For us it's a chilling signal and we should take warning.

What they're trying to tell us is we'd better stop depending on oil for so many uses. Oil should be used only when there is no practical alternative.

Unlike many nations, we're fortunate. We have a superabundance of coal that can be used instead of precious oil for many of our energy needs.

We're sitting on half the world's known supply of coal—enough for over 500 years.

It may well be impossible for us to become totally independent. But certainly we can reduce our dependence on foreign fuel.

We as a nation must make a commitment to coal. Face and solve any problems that exist.

And ask not if coal has a place in America's future, for coal is America's future. But ask only what needs to be done, by reasonable men, to use this vast and valuable asset.

Let's end this senseless delay. Let's pull our foot off the brake and get America going.   Now!

American Electric Power Company, Inc.

Subsidiaries:
Appalachian Power Co., Indiana & Michigan Electric Co., Kentucky Power Co., Kingsport Power Co., Michigan Power Co., Ohio Power Co., Wheeling Electric Co.

AT&T Long Distance, 1970 ◀◀   Bendix Corporation, 1970 ◀   American Electric Power Company, 1974

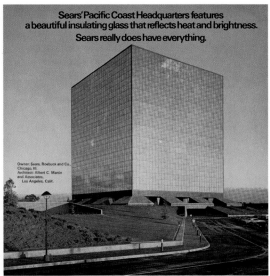

PPG Industries Glass, 1973

PPG Industries Glass, 1970

PPG GLASS: A SPECTACULAR MATERIAL THAT MANAGES ENERGY.

PPG Industries Glass, 1978

Seriously.

LIFE didn't think last summer's Woodstock Festival was so silly. We sent our reporters and photographers to the Woodstock hills...and ended up with an entire issue devoted to the b rock concert in history.

And we don't see anything silly about college students speaking their minds. We take what say...about the war, about our cities, about our country ...and print it. Because a lot of it makes sense.

Which is the same conscientious way we handle all our stories. Whether they're about the friends of Prince Charles, the boom in astrology, or offbeat ideas in art.

There's nothing very silly about LIFE's low price either. 25 weeks of straight thinking and thorough reporting for just $2.95. Which is less than 12¢ an issue.

We'll even bill you later. After you've seen for yourself some serious coverage of the things that interest you.

Just send in the attached order card today while this bargain price is still in effect. Have y own copy of LIFE sent to you every week, and stay right on top of things.

Right where you should be.

What has Mr. Nixon ever really done for you?

Unless you want to see the civil rights gains of the 60's sabotaged further—or even wiped out—vote November 7 for George McGovern.

Richard Nixon is the one who went on nationwide television to arouse anti-busing prejudice. Richard Nixon has talked about the undesirability of "forced integration of the suburbs," as if the right of every American to a home of his choice is somehow a bad thing.

During the Nixon Administration black unemployment has almost doubled—up to 9.7%. Among Black and minority youth in poverty areas, unemployment is up to 40%. And after introducing with great fanfare his "Philadelphia Plan" for requiring government building contractors to hire more minority workers, Nixon backed away from enforcing it.

Mr. Nixon recently vetoed a Health, Education and Welfare Bill that included $15 million for the treatment and prevention of Sickle Cell Anemia.

George McGovern, on the other hand, has always been one of the most steadfast friends of human rights.

• McGovern has co-sponsored every major civil rights bill during his ten years in the Senate.
• McGovern has been for years the leader in the fight to end U.S. involvement in Vietnam—a war that has killed and maimed a disproportionate number of Black Americans.
• McGovern is the only Senator who has fully supported the substance of the Black Caucus Congressional Black Bill of Rights.
• McGovern was the only member of Congress besides Rep. John Conyers to join in the March Against Fear in Atlanta in May, 1970... accepting the personal invitation of Mrs. Martin Luther King.

• McGovern is the principal sponsor in the Senate of the bill to make Rev. Martin Luther King's birthday a national holiday.

If he has done all these things as a Senator, imagine what McGovern will do as President?

• McGovern is committed to the vigorous enforcement of civil rights laws to wipe out discrimination in jobs, schools, housing and voting rights.
• McGovern has pledged full participation of Blacks, Browns, women and young people on all levels of his administration.
• McGovern would urge enactment of a National Health Security Program to guarantee the best possible medical care for every American.

• McGovern has revealed a plan that will guarantee a decent job to every able-bodied person who wants to work... and a decent income for those who are unable to work, including the aged, children, dependent mothers, and the disabled.

• McGovern wants to make quality education available to all Americans. He has proposed an additional $15 billion in new aid to local school systems—to greatly improve education and reduce property taxes at the same time.

Is it any wonder that George McGovern is the choice of Mrs. Coretta King, Rep. Julian Bond, Rev. Ralph Abernathy, Rep. Walter E. Fauntroy, Mayor Richard G. Hatcher, Mayor Ken Gibson, Louis Stokes and William Clay.

All Americans have a big stake in this election. Vote Nov. 7 for George McGovern and Sargent Shriver.

Authorized and paid for by McGovern-Shriver Campaign Committee • 1910 K Street, N.W., Washington, D.C. 20006 • Marian Pearlman, Treasurer

George McGovern, 1974

Look who reads the Bible.

It can make things work for you.
It's that kind of book.
Read your Bible. You'll see.
If you don't have a Bible of your own, we'll send you one for a dollar.
Hard cover and everything.
Just one should do it.
The Bible lasts a long time.

National Bible Week Committee
P.O. Box 1170, Ansonia Station
New York, New York 10023

Good. I'm sending you one dollar.
Please send me one Bible.

NAME
ADDRESS
CITY   STATE   ZIP

30th Annual National Bible Week, November 22-29, 1970. An interfaith effort.

The Blues Image, Atco Records

National Bible Week Committee, 1970

You'd expect it from National. The Affordable *Solar-Assisted* Homes.

They can cut your energy costs for space and water heating and cooling up to 60%*

*compared to an all-electric home.

The practical way to own a new energy-saving home that starts saving you money from the very first day.

Here. Today... is a truly sensible answer to tomorrow's higher fuel costs. Homes that combine the economies of the sun with advanced energy-saving heating and cooling and insulation methods.

The result is a unique system: Revere's Sun Pride™ Water Heating System—the complete system for heating domestic water with solar energy; General Electric's Weathertron® Heat Pump with Climatuff™ Compressor—an electric system that cools without water, heating without burning fuel; STYROFOAM TG insulation sheathing—the unique insulation from The Dow Chemical Company covering

every square foot of wall (except door and window openings); National's own exclusive Thermo-Shield insulation system.

The energy-savings system is available in hundreds of floor plans in ranches, split-levels and two-story homes.

The energy savings can be significant. It's easy to prove it to yourself. Visit your National Homes Builder today.

*Based on an October, 1977 independent study of 42 cities using ASHRAE calculations comparing an 1181 sq. ft. ranch model on a crawlspace built to FHA Minimum Property Standards using electric resistance space and water heating and electric cooling with an identical house containing the Affordable Solar-Assisted Home package. Data available upon request. Savings will vary depending on climate, home size, type, location and orientation, fuel rates and family size.

CALL TOLL FREE
for the name of your nearest
National Homes Builder.

800/621-8318
(In Illinois phone 800/972-8308)
Corporate Offices, Lafayette, IN 47902

MORE FAMILIES LIVE IN
NATIONAL HOMES
THAN ANY OTHER HOMES
IN THE WORLD

GENERAL ELECTRIC   THERMO-SHIELD   REVERE   STYROFOAM TG (Trademark of The Dow Chemical Company)

Life Magazine, 1970 ◄   *National Homes, 1978*

Thor Heyerdahl, Ra Voyage, 1970

"Sailing across the Atlantic we observed oil pollution on 43 out of 57 days"

"When I was sailing across the Atlantic on a reed boat I had my nose literally in the water. I saw things so one can see who travels by fast boat.

"Fifty miles off the bulge of Africa we found we could not brush our teeth in the seawater—it was covered with oil. We sailed through this mess for two days, and a week later ran into more.

Oil pollutes the fish we eat

"On a second raft trip we sailed through water filled with lumps of

oil for 43 out of 57 days.

Great whales and many fish which swim with their mouths open, filtering their food, are swallowing this pollution. Some of those fish we shall eat.

The seas will suffocate

"There are people who tell you that oil does not matter, that the sea can absorb and recycle all this pollution. I call them the Sandmen—they want to put you to sleep with calming words. *Don't listen!*

"Unless you and I—all of us—act now to stop the seas being overloaded with poisonous refuse, they will suffocate and die."

That was 1970, but it goes on today—Nantucket, Cape Cod and Delaware Bay—and you don't see it, except in the press.

That is why World Wildlife Fund is campaigning to save the life and resources of the seas—for our own sakes and those of our children.

You can help

Send for our free information kit or send your tax-deductible contribution to: World Wildlife Fund, Department U-1, 1319 18th Street, Northwest, Washington, D.C. 20036.

World Wildlife Fund

World Wildlife Fund, 1978

This is the tag you should look for even before you check the price tag.

The Herculon II* tag tells you what no price tag can.

That the manufacturer is no Johnny-come-lately. He's long been a trendsetter. A perennial fashion innovator. And proud of the reputation he's built.

The Herculon II tag tells you he doesn't mind working a bit harder to maintain that reputation. Putting in the extra effort it take to meet Herculon II standards. So his dresses or shirts or sweaters don't come out looking like anybody else's.

TUA MARKETING, INC.

1345 Avenue of the Americas, New York, New York 10019

HERCULON II

Piece of mind.

A tiny electronic brain, nestling near Ladybug.

An RCA integrated circuit with 1,300 transistors built in.

It can operate a watch, a pocket calculator, security alarm, automotive systems…replacing mechanical devices.

It's more reliable, accurate, economical, needs little power, doesn't pollute.

By 1985, such circuit chips may contain as many as a million transistors… making even today's technology look quaint.

Innovating in electronics.

From the beginning.

RCA

RCA Electronics, 1975

What's all this about Ecology?

It's child's play – and fun for adults, too – with Ecology Kits and Games.

The games are SMOG®, DIRTY WATER®, ECOLOGY® and POPULATION™. They challenge players of all ages to solve the crises and find the strategies of today's concerned world leaders. $10.00 each.

Ecology Kits help everyone from age 8 to adult uncover provocative natural mysteries. And beginning ecologists can prove their discoveries with fascinating experiments and projects. Eight different kits. $6.00 each.

The ecology kits and games are designed by Urban Systems – a team of ecology experts who think learning should be an adventure. And who care about the world our children will know.

BULLOCK'S · BUFFUM'S · MAY CO. · I. MAGNIN · F.A.O. SWARTZ · BROADWAY and better toy stores

 URBAN SYSTEMS INC.
1033 Massachusetts Ave.
Cambridge, Mass. 02138

Urban Systems Inc., 1971

When you sign something special, think of Textron.

Textron, Providence, Rhode Island 02903

Why? Because whenever you take pen in hand, you're likely to be writing with a fine instrument from Textron's Sheaffer Division—pens, ballpoints and precision pencils crafted in a proud tradition.

Think about it. Textron is Sheaffer writing instruments. And Gorham pewter, silver, china and crystal. And Talon zippers.

And the one thing they all have in common is the very uncommon products they are.

Textron
A COMPANY TO THINK ABOUT.

TUA Marketing, 1972 ◄   *Textron, 1975*

The phone company wants more installers like Alana MacFarlane.

Alana MacFarlane is a 20-year-old from San Rafael, California. She's one of our first women telephone installers. She won't be the last.

We also have several hundred male telephone operators. And a policy that there are no all-male or all-female jobs at the phone company.

We want the men and women of the telephone company to do what they want to do, and do best.

For example, Alana likes working outdoors. "I don't go for office routine," she said. "But as an installer, I get plenty of variety and a chance to move around."

Some people like to work with their hands, or, like Alana, get a kick out of working 20 feet up in the air.

Others like to drive trucks. Some we're helping to develop into good managers.

Today, when openings exist, local Bell Companies are offering applicants and present employees some jobs they may never have thought about before. We want to help all advance to the best of their abilities.

AT&T and your local Bell Company are equal opportunity employers.

AT&T Telephone Services, 1972

How come there's no Moscow Mercantile Exchange?

Millions of tons of potatoes, cabbage and other commodities change hands in the U.S.S.R. every year, but not a ruble's worth is traded on any futures market. In a regulated economy, the price of a head of cabbage is exactly what the government says it is—no more, no less. Does their system work? Apparently. Does it work as well as ours? You've got to be kidding.

CHICAGO MERCANTILE EXCHANGE
444 West Jackson Blvd., Chicago, Illinois 60606

Chicago Mercantile Exchange, 1974

▶ *U.S. Army National Guard, 1976*

The most important part-time job in America.

The New Minutemen of the Army Guard share a unique American heritage with William H. Carney. A Sergeant in the 54th Massachusetts Colored Infantry Regiment during the Civil War, Carney received the Medal of Honor for heroic devotion to duty during fierce fighting at Fort Wagner, S.C. on July 18, 1863.

Outstanding black Americans still protect our country and our communities in today's Army Guard, of course. One weekend a month thousands of these modern day citizen-soldiers come together all across the nation to train and sharpen their skills. And you can join them.

More than 400 career specialties are open to you. You'll earn good pay for learning one of them, too. About $45 for just one weekend a month to start.

And with every promotion there's a pay raise. Another thing, we're close to home.

Be one of The New Minutemen. Contact your local Army Guard Recruiter, complete and mail the attached coupon, or call toll free 800-638-7600 (except in Alaska, Hawaii, Puerto Rico, and the Virgin Islands). In Maryland call 301-728-3388.

ARMY NATIONAL GUARD
The Guard belongs.

When the World War II Vets came home there were bands, kisses, jobs and education for the asking.

Last year their sons came home from a war which was in many ways far worse. And they're getting cold shoulders, slammed doors, few jobs and less money for education, subsistence or anything else.

It's the basic things that hurt . . . the lack of money for rent or education or even food. But it's the little things that finally break you . . . like the late check that the VA says is due to some computer foul-up or the lack of transportation money to get to job interviews. And you don't want a public dole.

Our forgotten men can't wait. They cannot wait until it gets straightened out in Washington. That's why we've set up the Veteran's Emergency Fund. We won't be around next year asking for your money. We're just what we're called: an Emergency Fund. Set up right now to provide emergency subsistence to the Vietnam Vet while he gets on his own two feet again. Funding will be disbursed in the form of outright grants or short-term no-interest loans and will be administered by the non-profit Kharma Foundation.

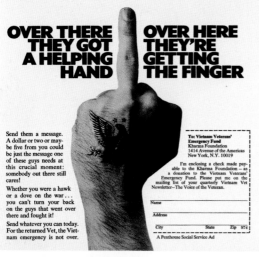

OVER THERE THEY GOT A HELPING HAND   OVER HERE THEY'RE GETTING THE FINGER

Send them a message. A dollar or two or maybe five from you could be just the message one of these guys needs at this crucial moment: somebody out there still cares!

Whether you were a hawk or a dove on the war . . . you can't turn your back on the guys that went over there and fought it!

Send whatever you can today. For the returned Vet, the Vietnam emergency is not over.

To: Vietnam Veterans' Emergency Fund
Kharma Foundation
1414 Avenue of the Americas
New York, N.Y. 10019

I'm enclosing a check made payable to the Kharma Foundation — as a donation to the Vietnam Veterans' Emergency Fund. Please put me on the mailing list of your quarterly Vietnam Vet Newsletter—The Voice of the Veteran.

Name

Address

City   State   Zip   974

A Penthouse Social Service Ad

Vietnam Veteran's Emergency Fund, 1974

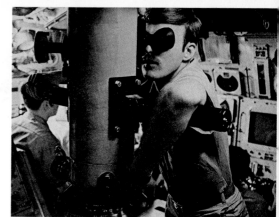

NAVY NUCLEAR PROPULSION.
THE FASTEST WAY UP IN NUCLEAR ENGINEERING.

If you want to get into nuclear engineering, start by getting into the Nuclear Navy.

The Navy operates more than half the reactors in America. So our nuclear training is the most comprehensive you can get. You start by earning your commission as a Navy Officer. Then we give you a year of advanced nuclear technology, training that would cost you thousands if you could get it in graduate school. During your career, you'll get practical, hands-on experience with our nuclear powered fleet. Maybe you'll work on a nuclear submarine, maybe a nuclear cruiser. But wherever you work, you'll really get to prove your worth–as a young Nuclear Propulsion Officer entrusted with the most advanced technical equipment known to man.

If that sounds like the kind of responsibility you're looking for, speak to your Navy recruiter. He can tell you if you qualify as a Nuclear Propulsion Officer Candidate. Or call toll free **800-841-8000.** (In Georgia, 800-342-5855.) Navy Nuclear Propulsion Officer. Some men wait for the future. He lives it now.

NAVY OFFICER.
IT'S NOT JUST A JOB, IT'S AN ADVENTURE.

U.S. Navy, 1977

U.S. Army, 1972

Is this your last summer for a summer job?

Summer jobs between high school years are good-time jobs. A little work, a lot of laughs, and a few extra bucks when you head back to school in September.

But the summer job after graduation is your last summer job. And if you're not going on to college this fall, consider a job in today's Army.

A job that teaches you a skill and pays you as you learn. You start at $288 a month. With free meals, housing, medical and dental care, and 30 days paid vacation each year.

It's a job that lets you live away from home and afford it. Not only in the States, but in places like Europe, Hawaii, Panama, and Alaska.

Finally, if after your 3-year enlistment you're interested in college, there's 36 months of financial assistance at the college of your choice.

If you'd like to know more about this unique combination of job-training, pay and benefits, see your Army Representative. Or send us the coupon.

Today's Army wants to join you.

Army Opportunities
Dept. 200, Hampton, Va. 23369
I'd like to know more about the job-training and promotion opportunities in today's Army.

Name   Date of birth
Address
City   County
State   Zip   Phone
Education

The day Bill told off his boss

Cleveland Institute of Electronics, 1970

How to tell your parents you want to join the Army.

You're graduating from high school and not going to college. And you're not really prepared for a job. You're not even certain you know what you want to do. Or can do.

Tell your parents you can find out in the Women's Army Corps. Find out which of the many fields you might do well in. Like medical, dental, personnel management, communications, stock control, data processing, or administrative procedures.

And tell them we'll train you for a career in that field. And pay you while you learn. At a starting salary of $288 a month. And since so many things in the Army are free—meals, housing, medical and dental care—you may save most of your salary.

Or spend it on the 30 days paid vacation we give you every year. Go almost anywhere in the world. Europe, Hawaii, the Far East, or any of those great places you've always wanted to see in the States. All at a very low cost.

Tell them that you can continue your education, too. Take special courses. Even go for your college degree. And that we'll pay for most of it.

Tell them that in today's Army you may discover abilities you never knew you had. And use them in a rewarding, responsible job. You'll find new friends. Meet people. Mature.

For more good reasons, see your local Army Representative. Or send us the coupon.

Today's Army wants to join you.

U.S. Army, 1972

U.S. Airforce National Guard, 1977

Radioactivity.
It's been in the family for generations.

In fact, scientists can tell us just how old our remote ancestors are by measuring the radioactivity still in the bones of prehistoric cave dwellers.

Radioactivity dating is possible because virtually everything on earth—food, air, water, man himself—is radioactive and always has been.

Obviously, radiation is nothing new. Using nuclear power plants to generate electricity isn't exactly new either.

We've been doing it for 15 years.

And experience has shown that a person living next door to a nuclear power plant for a year would be exposed to less additional radiation than by making one round-trip coast-to-coast flight.

Understanding that nuclear power plants are safe, clean places to make electricity is important, because the demand for electric energy continues to grow. And nuclear power is one of the best ways we have for meeting it.

Our country's ability to do the work that needs to be done will depend on an adequate supply of electricity. There's no time to waste. New generating facilities must be built, and built in a way compatible with our environment.

We'll continue working to do this. But we need your understanding today to meet tomorrow's needs.

The people at your Investor-Owned Electric Light and Power Companies:

For names of sponsoring companies, write to Power Companies, 1245 Avenue of the Americas, New York, New York 10019.

Olivetti Typewriters, 1970 ◄

Investor-Owned Electric Light & Power Companies, 1972

Consumer
Products
102

Andy Warhol's unfinished symphony.

We asked Andy Warhol to paint a picture of a Pioneer high fidelity receiver. He can't seem to finish. He says he gets so wrapped up in the beautiful sound of the subject that he can't concentrate on the way it looks.

Andy is a great artist, film-maker and journalist. And he's a man who appreciates great music. He knows you can't have great music unless you have great equipment.

That's why he owns Pioneer. As far as the portrait goes, he has our unfinished sympathy.

U.S. Pioneer Electronics Corp., 75 Oxford Drive, Moonachie, New Jersey 07074.
West: 13300 S. Estrella, Los Angeles 90248 / Midwest: 1500 Greenleaf, Elk Grove Village, Illinois 60007
Canada: S. H. Parker Co.

⊕ PIONEER®
when you want something better

Akai Stereo Equipment, 1974 ◄ *Pioneer Electronics, 1975*

► *General Electric Televisions, 1979*

INTRODUCING A REVOLUTIONARY BIG PICTURE COLOR TELEVISION.

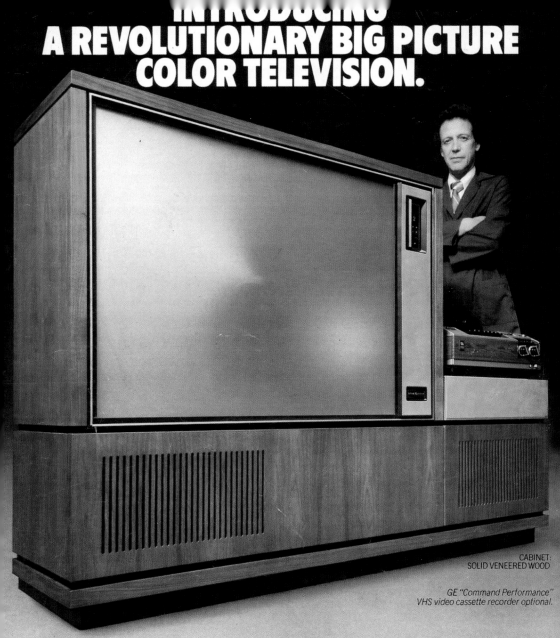

CABINET:
SOLID VENEERED WOOD

GE "Command Performance"
VHS video cassette recorder optional.

You're looking at the new General Electric Widescreen 1000. A super size color TV with a picture three times the size of a 25" diagonal console. A picture that makes you feel like you're at the movies. A set with the advanced performance features you expect from General Electric.

Like VIR. The Emmy award-winning color system that gives you realistic flesh tones, blue skies, green grass. Automatically adjusted by the broadcaster's signal on many programs. GE won the Emmy in 1977 for being the first to use VIR.

And electronic tuning. With the chairside convenience of random access remote control. So you can go from channel 2 to 83 instantly.

See this and other examples of General Electric leadership in television at your GE TV dealer.

THIS IS GE PERFORMANCE TELEVISION.

"We are dedicated to the philosophy of putting beautiful sound within everyone's reach. We have achieved this goal by creating and designing a spectrum of Audio Systems that are the ultimate in sophistication but simple to operate. Functionally designed yet exquisitely beautiful. A complete collection of Audio Systems that gives people the opportunity to enrich their lives with magnificent sound. This is why we're number one in stereo and Quadraphonic equipment in America."

Chairman and President
Morse Electro Products Corp.

Electrophonic

BALANCE

4D DISCRETE   SQ MATRIX   POWER

4D   ① ② ③ ④

Electrophonic presents: True compatible Quadraphonic 400 Watt I.P.P. Audio System plays D SQ-Matrix and Stereo with built-in 4 channel and 8-track tape, magnetic Garrard ch Super Sphere air suspension speaker system. This week only, Model MAG 487XP, special introd offer only $400 at leading department stores and Electrophonic dealers listed at right. After sal

"My $3000 lifesize VideoBeam® television has almost paid for itself in the beer my friends have brought me."

T. Barton Carter, Boston, Mass.
Advent VideoBeam owner since Feb. 1977

"I tell my friends they can come and watch basketball, hockey, football, whatever, anytime . . . as long as I don't run out of beer."

We taped a conversation with Barton Carter, teacher of communications law and sports freak, and this is what he said about his VideoBeam television, his friends, and what goes on at his place.

It's like being there.

"I'll have eight or ten people over for a basketball game. What with the immediacy and the way the VideoBeam picture sort of wraps around you and involves you, and all these people together . . . it gets pretty crazy. It's like being at the game.

"Actually what with the different camera perspectives you see more than you would at the game. It shows best in the stuff that goes on underneath the basket. You really see the elbows, people banging around. Anyone who says basketball isn't a contact sport hasn't seen it on VideoBeam. For instance you can see when Cowens gets really mad. All of a sudden there's an extra two feet around him. Nobody wants to get near him, not even his teammates. You wouldn't see that on the little tube. No way.

Better feel for the strategy.

"You can see what people are trying to do, not only what they're accomplishing. You can see when somebody is trying to get the ball around to the weak side, but they can't because somebody has cut off the passing lane. You get a better feel for the strategy of the coaches. You see who they're working on, you know, if they're trying to get

somebody down low, post a tall guard on a short one . . .

You "Feel" the contact.

"Of course, football more than any other sport shows the contact . . . in fact you feel the contact. You see one of these big guys come steaming down the field at full speed and he gets his legs cut out from under him, does a twist and falls, um, you can just feel it. You get that sometimes under the boards in basketball. You can just feel them hitting each other. It's more than just seeing it.

"And if you've got eight or ten people watching it's magnified. And if they're rooting for different teams . . . oh boy . . . I'm thinking of hiring a bouncer for the next game."

VideoBeam television projects brilliant color TV pictures from regular broadcasts and from video cassette recorders on to a six-foot diagonal screen. If you would like to know more and see a demonstration return the coupon, or call toll free 800-225-1035 (in Massachusetts call Customer Relations at (617) 661-9500) for brochures and the name and address of your nearest dealer.

Actual closed circuit television picture.

Advent's VideoBeam® Television
It's beyond TV.

Advent Corporation, 195 Albany Street, Cambridge, Mass. 02139 (617) 661-9500

No two people ever really enjoy all the same things. What turns one on may very well turn the other off. (Which is what happens to your stereo system during Marcus Welby.)

But with Koss Stereophones, you can live and let live. Because both can be turned on at the same time. As loud as you want, without disturbing the other.

And that should be music to any man's ears.

Fact is, nothing else quite matches the sound you hear with Koss Stereophones.

It extends the bass, treble and mid-range of your favorite music farther than the most expensive speaker system.

So you hear more of your music and none of the late show.

If you'd like to see more, write for our free full-color catalog, c/o Virginia Lamm, Dept. ES-O.

And if you'd like to hear the Sound of Koss, try a set at your favorite Stereo Dealer or Department Store . . . from $19.95 to $150. It's a small price to pay for a little peace.

ⓚKOSS STEREOPHONES

Koss Corporation, 4129 N. Port Washington Ave., Milwaukee, Wis. 53212
Koss International Ltd. Via Valtorta, 21 20127, Milan, Italy

Live and let live

Koss Stereophones, 1971

▶ *JVC Videosphere Televisions, 1972*

We made the Videosphere look the way it does because when your TV's off you still have to look at it.

The Videosphere by JVC is a new way of looking at television. As part of the total environment of a room.

You don't watch TV all the time. And your television should be just as much a part of the room when it's off as it is when it's on.

But don't get the idea that styling is the only thing futuristic about the Videosphere. Because it isn't.

An advanced Electronic Expander Circuit makes sure you get a clear picture, no matter where you are. And this is important. Because the Videosphere, besides looking great anywhere, can also go anywhere. It's portable. And we do mean portable. It weighs less than 12 pounds. And it's as much at home outdoors as it is indoors.

As a matter of fact, the Videosphere is also available in another model with a clock. So you can wake up to the same thing you're going to sleep with now. Television.

The Videosphere by JVC. It looks better off than most TV's look when they're on.

JVC

For those nights you want everything to be just right...

Let the luscious sound of soft music from your superb new stereo system help you set the mood . . . reveal your taste, your style, your deepest feelings to him. You can create the most romantic atmosphere with this beautiful, contemporary Apollo system from Electrophonic.

You'll let him know, too, that you're involved in the "today" sound. Because Electrophonic gives you 200 Watts of purring power. Air-Suspension speakers that catch every subtle whisper. FET/IC Circuitry for instant "on". An 8-track tape player, an AM/FM/FM-stereo radio and a Garrard Record Changer with cueing control, diamond stylus.

This fabulous Electrophonic stereo system gives you even more. It's equipped with a Speaker Matrix Switch to go all the way to full four-channel sound with the addition of two speakers. And the Apollo series is also available with recording facility so you can create your own professional tapes at the push of a button.

You can choose which of the smart decorator colors will blend with your own decor . . . pale, pale champagne or very cool blue . . . at fine department stores in the U.S. and Canada.

All this glamour and mood-setting can be yours—and his—now, so why wait? Tonight might be one of those nights.

Electrophonic AMERICA'S LARGEST STEREO MANUFACTURER

Electrophonic Stereos, 1974

▶ RCA Electronics, 1971   ▶ ▶ Panasonic Electronics, 1973

SOUNDS OF SPRING

RCA's exciting styles for spring gift giving.

Just in time for Mother's Day, Father's Day, a June bride or the graduate.
Whatever the occasion this spring, we'll have you covered with
a radio, phonograph or tape instrument.
Look for the Sounds of Spring at your RCA dealer.
He's all abloom with gift ideas.

Model RZG-354.
Portable AM radio
with compass and
flashlight, $39.95.*

Model VPP-48. Portable phonograph with
speakers that separate to 20 feet, $79.95.*

Model
RZD-311.
Decorator AM
clock radio,
$29.95.*

Model YZB-386.
AC/DC tape
recorder/player
and FM-AM
radio combination,
$89.95.*

Model RZS-476.
FM/AM cube
with digital clock,
lighted dial and
wakeup features, $49.95.*

Model RZS-335.
FM/AM radio with clock
and calendar, $50.00.*

New vibrations from an old master.

RCA

The Crazy C
They evei

Crazy is how they look. Fun-crazy. But when you listen to them, you discover that the Crazy Color Portables are very down to earth. Even though the music they make is out of this world.

And so are the shapes. Like an AM shape that twists and turns and closes around your little wrist. The Toot-A-Loop™ Model R-72. Or another AM shape that turns, swings and dangles from your little finger. The Ball 'n Chain™ Model R-70.

You can drink in melodies from the Music Mug™ Model R-63. Or truck to funky fifties golden oldies on our hip square, the Musicube™ Model R-47A. Or you might prefer to roll in FM and AM. With the Rolling Tone™ Model RF-93.

If they're too eccentric for you, you can get Crazy Color Portable radios in a variety of half-crazy, mildly

Fun for all ages.

R-72 original design by J. M. Wilmin

or Portables.
play music.

neurotic and completely straight shapes.

And if you want to make your own kind of music, there's Take 'n Tape™ Model RQ-711S. The portable cassette recorder that looks like something out of 2001.

And for your records, there are Funnygraphs™ Yuk, yuk. That look like space-age waffle irons.

Model SG-200A plays 33 and 45 rpm waffles. While Model SG-400A also cooks up delicious AM.

What's more, you can start hearing things, as well as seeing them, immediately. Because all the Crazy Color Portables come with Panasonic batteries.

The Panasonic Crazy Color Portables. They were made to be seen. And heard.

Gifts for all seasons.

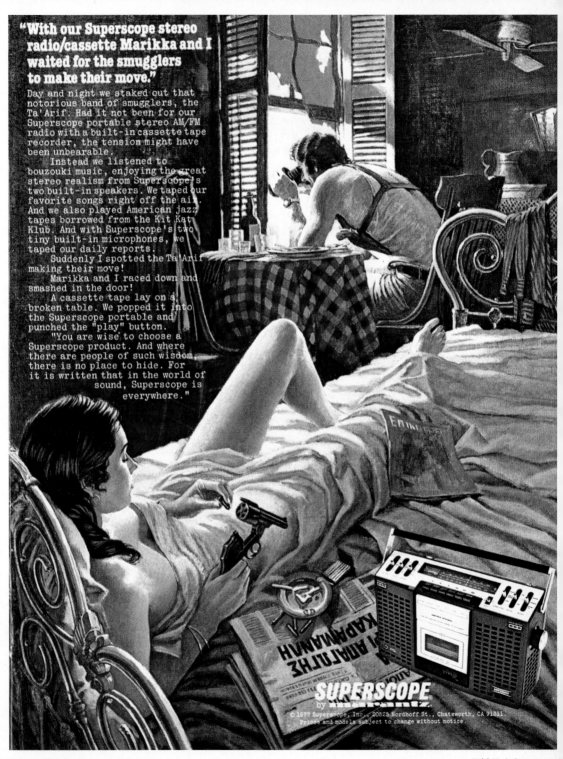

"**With our Superscope stereo radio/cassette Marikka and I waited for the smugglers to make their move.**"

Day and night we staked out that notorious band of smugglers, the Ta'Arif. Had it not been for our Superscope portable stereo AM/FM radio with a built-in cassette tape recorder, the tension might have been unbearable.

Instead we listened to bouzouki music, enjoying the great stereo realism from Superscope's two built-in speakers. We taped our favorite songs right off the air. And we also played American jazz tapes borrowed from the Kit Kat Klub. And with Superscope's two tiny built-in microphones, we taped our daily reports.

Suddenly I spotted the Ta'Arif making their move!

Marikka and I raced down and smashed in the door!

A cassette tape lay on a broken table. We popped it into the Superscope portable and punched the "play" button.

"You are wise to choose a Superscope product. And where there are people of such wisdom, there is no place to hide. For it is written that in the world of sound, Superscope is everywhere."

SUPERSCOPE
by marantz.

© 1977 Superscope, Inc., 20525 Nordhoff St., Chatsworth, CA 91311.
Prices and models subject to change without notice.

Superscope Stereos, 1977

▶ *Kodak Movie Cameras, 1973*

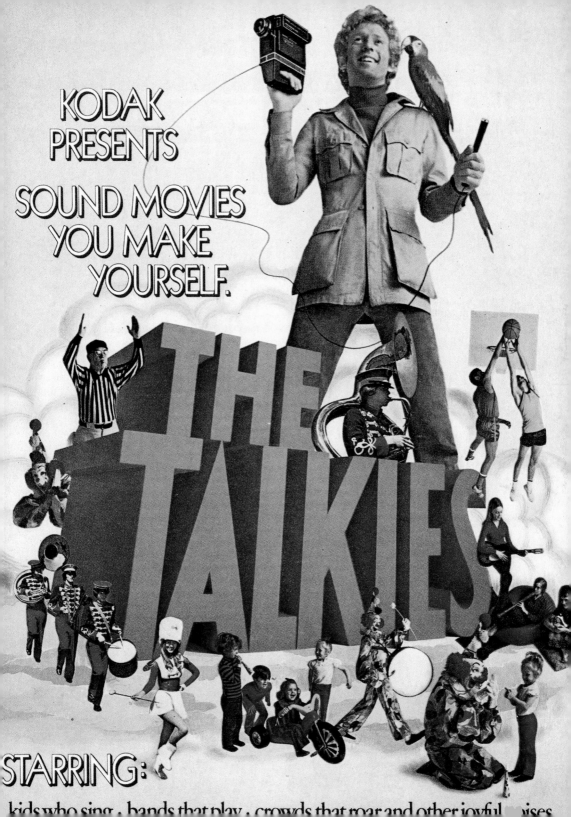

I choose my friends very carefully.

Very often, a phone is indeed like a friend. And now you can make it even more so.

There are all sorts of shapes and colors and styles of Bell telephones to choose from, together with all kinds of customized services.

So you can choose a phone you find amusing. Or one that's dashing. Or one you can just feel comfortable with. In short, you can choose a phone that's genuinely you, and still get a phone that's genuine Bell.

A friend you can like, and a friend you can trust.

⊕ Bell System

BE CHOOSEY

Reach out.
Reach out and touch someone.

Feeling fit, and all's right with the world? Then how about spreading that sunshine to a faraway friend? You can bet your leotards a simple phone call will really brighten her day. So get in touch. That phone call can keep a faraway friend close. Reach out and touch someone who's waiting to share your day.

Ⓐ Bell System

Bell System Telephones, 1979

For me, the choice was obvious.

There's a big choice in telephones these days. But the choice doesn't have to be difficult.

To find the right style and the right quality, just come right to Bell.

Because Bell telephones give you all sorts of shapes and colors and styles to choose from.

All Bell quality. And all kinds of customized calling services as well.

So, you can get a phone that's genuinely you, and still get a phone that's genuine Bell.

What could be more obvious?

Ⓐ Bell System

BE CHOOSEY

Bell System Telephones, 1978

1876

As we celebrate the nation's 200th anniversary, the take pride in the telephone's contribution to We intend to continue working–to keep

Bell System Telephones, 1978 ◀

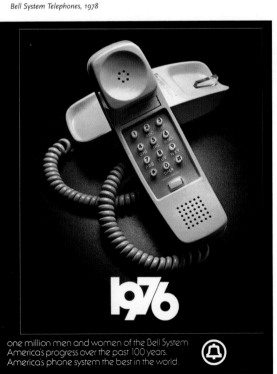

1976

one million men and women of the Bell System America's progress over the past 100 years. America's phone system the best in the world.

Ⓐ

Bell System Telephones, 1976

117

Rollei Cameras, 1977

Our Rollei 35: A camera you can wear anywhere.

Cup our Rollei 35S in the palm of your hand. Wonder how Rollei could pack such a high-performance optical system into such a compact space. Experiment with the extra-ordinary match-needle metering. Listen to the smooth, quiet operation of our shutter. Notice how the 35S accepts today's new 35mm, high-speed films. Then discover the big, beautiful photos produced by this beautiful, little camera. The Rollei 35S: Ask to see it at any Rollei dealer.

Rollei

Kodak Ektralite Camera, 1979

The Kodak Ektralite 10 camera has a convenient built-in electronic flash to catch all the action.

READY IN A FLASH!

- Convenience of built-in flash.
- Aim-and-shoot simplicity.
- The flash stops the action. 1/1000th of a second freezes just about anything or anybody.
- Dive into a fun camera... get the Ektralite 10.

©Eastman Kodak Company, 1979

Kodak Ektralite™ 10 Can Do.
camera

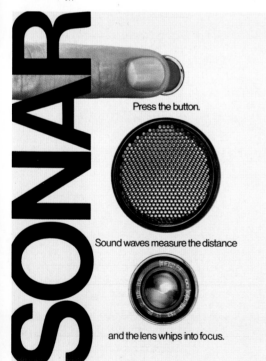

Polaroid Sonar Camera, 1978

SONAR

Press the button.

Sound waves measure the distance

and the lens whips into focus.

Polaroid Sonar Camera, 1978

©1978 Polaroid Corporation "Polaroid" "SX-70" and "Pronto" "SONAR OneStep"

Polaroid introduces Sonar automatic focusing.

Life doesn't just sit there waiting for you to focus. So Polaroid has invented a way for sonar to focus for you auto-matically. You press one button, and that's all. Within a split second, inaudible sound waves dart to the subject and back, and the lens whips into focus. With Polaroid's new Sonar OneStep Land cameras, you can get sharp, precisely focused pictures every time. And see them in minutes.

The Sonar OneSteps from 99.95*
OneSteps. The World's Simplest Cameras.
*Suggested list Pronto SONAR OneStep

NO DOUBT ABOUT IT.

No flash batteries to worry about. Just pop on a self-powered magicube.

If you try to use a used-up magicube, the camera gives you an automatic no-no.

No threading. Just drop in the film cartridge.

No settings. Just aim and shoot.

No doubt about it. The trim, slim Kodak Instamatic X-15 camera is a joy to use.

Ask about the X-15 in the extra-value Kodak Smile Saver kit, less than $25. Limited time only.

KODAK MAKES YOUR PICTURES COUNT

Kodak Instamatic Camera, 1971

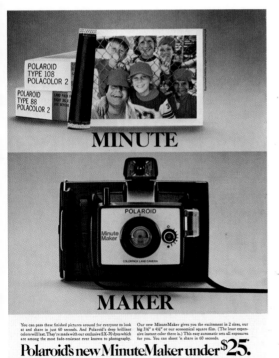

MINUTE

MAKER

You can pass these finished pictures around for everyone to look at and share in just 60 seconds. And Polaroid's deep brilliant colors will last. They're made with our exclusive SX-70 dyes which are among the most fade-resistant ever known to photography.

Our new MinuteMaker gives you the excitement in 2 sizes, our big 3¼" x 4½" or our economical square film. (The least expensive instant color there is.) This easy automatic sets all exposures for you. You can shoot 'n share in 60 seconds.

Polaroid's new MinuteMaker under $25.

Suggested List Price. © 1977 Polaroid Corporation. "Polaroid" "SX-70" and Minute Maker™

Polaroid MinuteMaker Camera, 1977

It was only fitting that this camera be bound in fine leather.

By all criteria, the SX-70 Alpha 1 is the unique single-lens reflex camera. Such a camera should also look distinctive. So we bound it in fine leather, as one binds a classic book, and set it off with a velvety chrome finish. It folds to about 1" x 4" x 7" so you can carry it gracefully from your shoulder or easily in your pocket. Inside, its sophisticated optics let you focus through the picture-taking lens to as close as 10.4".

You can take instant portraits, sequential pictures as fast as every 1½ seconds, daylight flash pictures, even automatic time exposures to 14 seconds. The Polaroid SX-70 Alpha 1 Land Camera.

Polaroid's SX-70 Alpha 1

© 1977 Polaroid Corporation

Polaroid SX-70 Alpha Camera, 1971 ▶ *Depraz-Faure Watches, 1971*

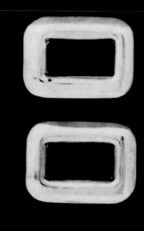

19.95 • Water and shock-resistant
Anti-magnetic • Guaranteed • Mod Band Extra
Other models available • See your local dealer

Some people know how to live.

They always seem to have a better time. Whether it's in New York or Marrakesh, Beirut or Paris. They entertain the same way they live. With a feeling for what's best in life. A desire for perfection and the ultimate in quality. Their tables show it. Warm with the glow of the world's finest china—Lenox. Alive with the sparkle of hand-blown Lenox Crystal. It's a world where second best just won't do.

LENOX
CHINA · CRYSTAL

For free pattern booklet write Lenox Inc., Trenton, N.J. 08605. 5-piece place setting of Lenox China; $24.95 to $85.00. 3-piece place setting

Your first microwave oven should be a Magic Chef.

Here's why: Every day, every meal, you'll save time with your Magic Chef microwave oven. With conveniences like the Magitrol Defroster that lets you dial the amount of microwave energy you need. So your frozen breakfast rolls taste the way the baker intended them to. So your hamburger isn't frozen in the center and burnt on the outside.

Colorful. Magic Chef has microwave ovens in popular kitchen appliance colors. So you can match your other appliances.

Clean. Cool microwave cooking means easier cleanups. And most of our ovens have stainless steel walls and a sealed-in ceramic shelf that wipes clean with just a sponge.

Budget-saving. Because you can reheat leftovers in minutes. Without drying them out. And because most families can do a full year's microwave cooking for less than $7.

American-Made. By Magic Chef. Makers of famous gas and electric ranges. One more reason that our complete selection of microwave ovens is a food lover's dream. Magic Chef, Cleveland, Tennessee.

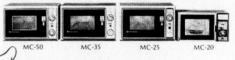

MC-50   MC-35   MC-25   MC-20

Magic Chef®
Cooking experts since 1924

Model MC50 shown

You've got a lifestyle.
The Beauty-Makers can help you live it.

You work. You keep house. You go to school. Maybe you're into yoga. That's okay. Because that's your lifestyle. And you want to look great every minute. We want you to. We being the people who make the Beauty-Makers. General Electric.

An hour to meet him, and your hair's a wreck. GE's Speedsetter to the rescue. With 20 tangle-free rollers that make setting panic free. Sets hair dry, with mist or with a conditioner.

Lifestyle.
We're with yours.
GENERAL (GE) ELECTRIC

He's coming for dinner, and you've just washed your hair. Under GE's Speed Dryer you go. Besides being fast, GE's Speed Dryer has Touch 'n Tilt. Touch, it tilts so you can do other things. Like type with two hands.

You like your hair the way it is, "natural." GE's new styling dryer will dry curly or straight hair, style it the way you want. High-powered. Handy (ours has a special easy-to-hold handle) so you can do other things. Like type with two fingers.

You're a travel nut. Meet GE's soft-bonnet dryer. Comes in its own carrying case like good, lightweight luggage. With two styling combs and a brush attachment.

The Beauty-Makers

Lenox Tablewares, 1971 ◄ ◄   *Magic Chef Microwave Oven, 1974* ◄   *General Electric Hair Styling Products, 1972*

My generation's got a charm of its own.

Master Jeweler

Charms and bracelets in the golden manner of Monet. Charms, $3 to $7.50. Bracelets, $3 to $15. At all fine stores.

All of a sudden jewelry isn't just a ring or two, a bracelet, and maybe a pair of earrings. It's a ring or nine or ten, bracelets up to here, and earrings, earrings, earrings. Enter Buxton. With more than thirty different kinds of jewelry boxes in almost every color you can think of. From $3.50.

Misty $8.00

Louise $15.00

Gaitor Baitor $12.50

Conquistador $25.00

BUXTON

All of a sudden jewelry boxes don't seem so stupid.

Monet Jewelers, 1973 ◄ *Buxton Jewelry Boxes, 1970* ► *Mattel Hug 'N Talk Dolls, 1978*

More Major League players wear Rawlings gloves than any other kind. Players like Brooks Robinson, Johnny Bench and Billy Williams. A few want minor customizing. But all wear, basically, the same Rawlings gloves you can buy in the store.

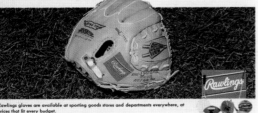

Rawlings gloves are available at sporting goods stores and departments everywhere, at prices that fit every budget.

Johnny Bench, Brooks Robinson and Billy Williams are members of Rawlings Pro Advisory Staff.
Rawlings Sporting Goods Company • Division of A.T.O Inc. • 2300 Delmar Blvd. • St. Louis, Mo. 63166

"THE MARK OF A PRO"

Rawlings Gloves, 1971

Every good cook has to start somewhere.

For her, there's no thrill quite like when she bakes that first Betty Crocker chocolate cake in her Easy-Bake Oven.

More than all the fun she'll have, Easy-Bake is a great way for her to create love in warm little bites.

Easy-Bake has built-in safety features, is U.L. approved and bakes with two ordinary light bulbs. And comes with real Betty Crocker mixes.

Easy-Bake. Because she'll love it.

Easy-Bake Oven from Kenner

© General Mills Fun Group, Inc.

Easy-Bake Oven, 1973

NeRF Toys

NeRF BALL
All kids love the world's first indoor ball, made of incredibly soft foam. In 2 sizes, Regular and Super.

NeRFOOP™
A sporty version that lets you shoot baskets indoors without damaging anything. Hoop and net not included.

NeRF FOOTBALL
Made of heavier foam, with a tough, protective skin for outdoors. You can really grip into it and make fantastic catches!

NeRF·MOBiLe™
Soft new toy cars, so cuddly that little children can take them to bed! Well-built, to roll like crazy, even over carpeting. Can't make noise or hurt furniture. Made of colorful, nontoxic Nerf foam with extra-strong wheels. Four snappy classics: Old Timer, Racer, Bug, and Sedan. Great fun for ages 3 to 6.

MONOPOLY® (Standard)
Kids and grown-ups love to buy, sell, swap real estate, build houses and hotels, collect rents, and merrily bankrupt each other in the world's most popular board game. Ages 8 to adult, 2 to 8 players.

MONOPOLY® (Better Edition)
Contains heavier board, extra equipment, plus special molded Banker's Tray which holds the money, houses, hotels and title cards neatly and conveniently. Ages 8 to adult, 2 to 10 players.

8

Playmobil Toys, 1978 ◄◄   *Chatham Blankets, 1976* ◄   *Nerf Toys and Monopoly Game, 1973*

SUPERMAN
A Collection of Records & Books

A SUPER ENCYCLOPEDIA OF THE SUPERHERO!

THE GREAT **SUPERMAN** BOOK

MICHAEL L. FLEISHER

★ OVER 1,000 ENTRIES
★ 472 ILLUSTRATIONS
★ A BOOK-LENGTH BIOGRAPHY OF SUPERMAN
★ STORY LINES OF MORE THAN 1,000 SUPERMAN ADVENTURES

★ EVERY FACT, ILLUSTRATION AND QUOTATION DRAWN DIRECTLY FROM THE COMICS!

THE GREAT SUPER-MAN BOOK A super encyclopedia of the greatest super hero in American mythology. From A-Z, you will find everything that you ever wanted to know about Krypton's child. 1000 entries, a full length biography, over 472 illustrations, and over 1000 story lines. Never before has the Super-man story been so thoroughly researched, catalogued and compiled. It stands as a monument to both fun and scholarship. Softcover format! #21343/$8.95

SUPERMAN 1930-1970 386 p. hardcover of Superman's adventures from origins to present! 3 color sections! #2145/$8.95

SUPERMAN'S FIRST EDITION Full color reproduction of the famous first edition! A 13"x10" softcover only . . . #21351/$2.00

SUPERMAN RADIO BROADCAST The original Superman radio broadcast from the golden age of radio! 12", 33 1/3 L.P. #2328/$6.95

SUPERMAN ADVENTURE RECORD 3 Superman action adventures on one stupendous 12", 33 1/3 L.P. Full color cover! #2397/$2.98

SUPERMAN ADVENTURE RECORD 4 super action packed Superman adventures on this 12", 33 1/3 L.P. Full color cover! #2396/$2.98

SUPERMAN RECORD & BOOK SET Full color illustrated book and a 12", 33 1/3 L.P. sound track to go with the book! #2398/$3.98

MAKING OF SUPERMAN How the film was made with the most awesome technology ever! #21341/$2.25

SUPERMAN QUIZ BOOK The official quiz book of all Superman facts and legends! #21340/$1.95

SUPERMAN: LAST SON OF KRYPTON Superman's story in novel form & 16 pages of photos! #21352/$2.50

AMAZING WORLD OF SU-PERMAN Oversize softback with special bonus map of Krypton! #21154/$2.98

READ THE BOOKS! LISTEN TO THE RECORDS! THE GREATEST ACTION-FILM EVER MADE! SUPERMAN THE WORLD'S #1 SUPERHERO

DC Comics Inc. 1978

To order any of these items, please see last page of this magazine for convenient RUSH ORDER FORM.

Superman Products, 1979

▶ *Star Wars Fan Club, 1978*

STAR WARS

The Raleigh forecast for Spring sees something good for everyone. Read on and see which Raleigh the stars have in store for you. It could be the blazing Raleigh Chopper® 3-speed, 5-speed, or the really spaced out new 10-speed rig with dual stick shift. On the other hand it could be one of the Raleigh 10-speed lightweights. But your future looks bright on a Raleigh.

RALEIGH FUNSCOPE

ARIES (March 21-April 19)— You are apt to be too serious. This is a good time to get out of yourself and head for good times on a Raleigh Chopper.

TAURUS (April 20-May 20)— You dig the country. A Raleigh Chopper with its short-thrust Split T-Bar power control is a great way to get around.

GEMINI (May 21-June 21) — You'd prefer more than one of everything. The new 10-speed Raleigh Chopper with dual stick shift could make you very happy.

CANCER (June 22-July 23) You are tradition bound with a keen imagination. The old-world craftsmanship and the performance of a 10-speed lightweight fits your nature.

LEO (July 24-August 23)— You tend to drift from person to person. A Raleigh 10-speed lightweight would be a great way to get from one to another.

VIRGO (August 24-September 23)— You stand for purity and perfection. Sit on a Raleigh 10-speed Chopper with double stick shift and third shift to "lock in" on any speed.

LIBRA (September 24-October 23)— You are a lover of harmony. Chopper's L-bucket Dragster Saddle will keep you in tune with the road.

SCORPIO (October 24-November 22)— At heart you are an adventurer. A Raleigh 10-speed lightweight should get you in and out in a hurry.

SAGITTARIUS (November 23-December 22)— You shun the conventional. Raleigh Chopper with racer-height vinyl-padded roll bar is as original as you are.

CAPRICORN (December 23-January 20)— You have both feet on the ground. Try putting them on a Raleigh Chopper and really letting go.

AQUARIUS (January 21-February 19)— You are usually ahead of others. So you probably already have a Raleigh Chopper. Well, you could try the lightweight model.

PISCES (February 20-March 20)— Your sensitive nature makes you cringe over low quality. Raleighs are made to the highest standards.

By now you've probably made up your mind to go see a dealer and test drive a Raleigh. If not send 25¢ for our new catalog to: Raleigh Industries of America, BL 71, 1168 Commonwealth Ave., Boston, Mass. 02134.

RALEIGH
NOTHING BETTER CAN BE SAID OF A BICYCLE

Made in England...serviced throughout America...guaranteed around the world.

Raleigh Bikes, 1971

Fuji Bikes, 1976

Murray Bikes, 1971

Schwinn Bikes, 1971

Schwinn Bikes, 1974

Cadillac Skateboard Wheels, 1974

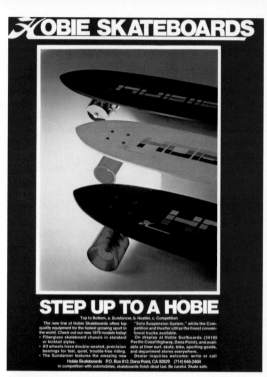

Hobie Skateboards, 1976

Joseph T. Walker Skateboards, 1976

Squirt Boogie Boards, 1978   ▶ *National Lampoon Magazine, 1970*

The Masses Are Revolting!

NATIONAL LAMPOON

... wouldn't you agree? All across the nation, the Forces of Formica and the Demagogues of Doublethink are determined to overthrow your sanity and your lunch.

Why not insulate yourself from this rather off-putting generation with a protective barricade of *National Lampoons?* Each month, you can hole up in your trendy chateau, put your feet up on an accommodating serf and quietly giggle at the entire mess with the help of our remarkable publication. Every issue of the *National Lampoon* slugs it out with a particular aspect of this annoying century, everything from politics to puberty. Designed to foil the Fascists and clot those bleeding hearts, the *National Lampoon* gives you a little perspective on these chicken-in-a-basket-case times.

Sound like fun? Well, you're wrong, it will be.

Just send Louise the Computer the very interesting coupon on this page along with $5.95 of your boring old money and we'll replace them with a full year of brand new chuckles 'n' boffs. Coming issues include Bad Taste, Paranoia, Show Biz, Politics and The Future!

Just $5.95 (the price of a single tie clip!) brings you monthly protection from those maddening maniacs determined to drive you out of your mind and into a straight-jacket.

Gay Bob Doll, 1978

Growers Choice Marijuana Fertilizer, 1978

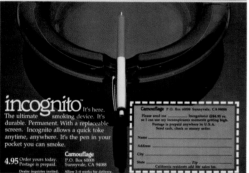

Camouflage Smoking Gear, 1977

Hell's Angels Apparel, 1977

Psilocybin Mushroom Cultivator's Bible, 1977

Mail-Order Smoking Gear, 1977

U.S. Bongs, 1977

▶ *Pioneer Speakers, 1974*

Pioneer High

idelity.

.oud

and

Clear.

"I am *precisely* three inches high," said the Caterpillar, "though I frequently become much higher."

"With that magic mushroom!" Alice asked eagerly.

"With music!" retorted the Caterpillar, conjuring visions of Fender® guitars and matching amplifiers. "I play inhumanly hot licks on my Stratocaster® and back myself with everything else."

"But *I* have only *two* arms," sighed Alice. "If I am to reach new heights on a Strat, I shall need your backing on electric bass!"

"On a *Fender!*" smiled the Caterpillar. "Or two or three. I should much rather get *my* hands on what TV concert bassmen play."

"And of course," Alice sang out . . . "*9 out of 10 pick a Fender bass!*"*

For a full-color poster of this ad, send $1 to: Fender, Box 3410, Dept. 175, Fullerton, CA 92634.

*Source: National Marketing Research of California, 1974.

CBS Musical Instruments
A Division of CBS Inc.

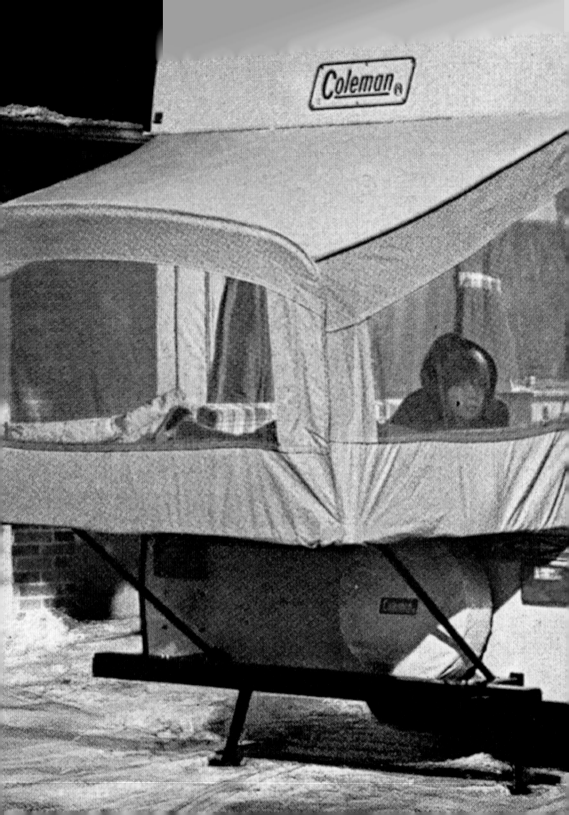

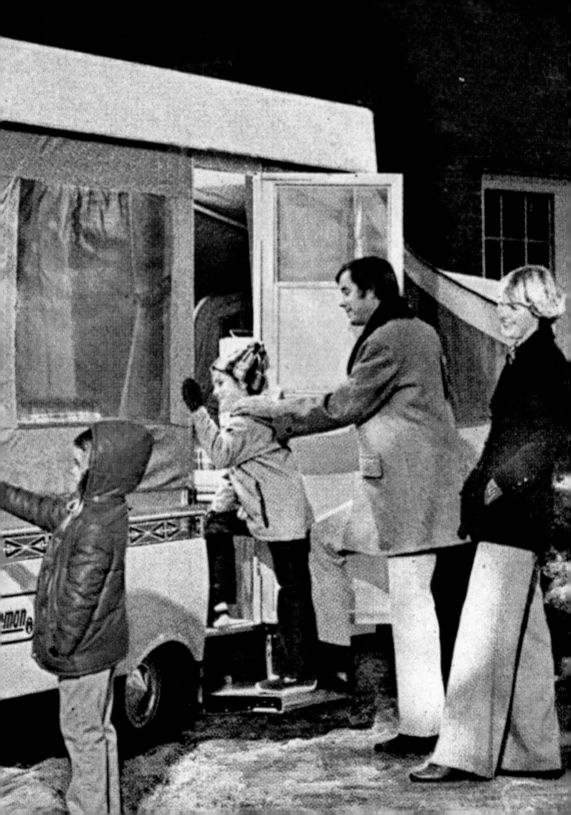

Crest Toothpaste, 1971

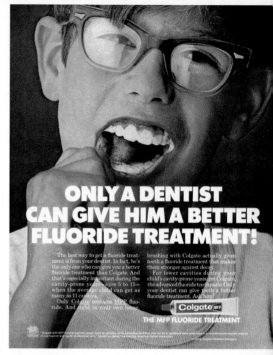

Colgate Toothpaste, 1972

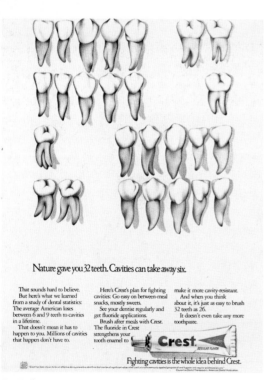

Crest Toothpaste, 1972

Palmolive Dishwashing Liquid, 1971   ▶ Monster Vitamins, 1975

Turn on a tan with *Johnson's*.

It's summer baby.

The pale, romantic heroine is out. The tan, romantic heroine is in. Be one, a bronze and beautiful one, by turning on a tan with *Johnson's* Baby Oil. It makes those long summer rays tan deep. And the deeper the tan, the longer it'll last after summer is gone. What's more, after sun bathing, bathing yourself in baby oil keeps your skin moist and supple.

It's the same pure oil your mother used to keep your skin soft and smooth when you were a baby. Just smooth it on and let the sun do its thing. But don't overdo it. (Remember, baby oil has no sunscreens, so you should take a little less sun than with cover-up lotions and creams.) Turn on a tan, baby. And you'll turn on your hero.

Ultra Brite Toothpaste, 1975 ◄

Johnson's Baby Oil, 1971

The look
is skin
by Jergens.

*Jergens not only
softens more hands,
but more elbows,
knees, and skin
all over than the
next 6 lotions
put together.
The Soft 1*

Fashions by Bill Blass.

Jergens Lotion, 1970

Mrs. Douglas Gian can compete with her
daughter's "Little Girl Look."

She helps keep her complexion
young looking with pure, mild Ivory.

IVORY
SOAP

More doctors recommend Ivory
99 44/100% pure® it floats®

Mrs. Douglas Gian of Elmsford, New York, and her daughter, Deborah. Photographed by Scavullo.

Ivory Soap, 1970

Touch the skin on your breast and see what GREAT SKIN can do for your face.

Have you ever noticed how baby smooth and soft the skin on your breast feels? That's because you keep this skin covered. So the natural moisture stays near the surface. It doesn't get dried out the way your facial skin does.

This is why the skin on your face can benefit dramatically from Great Skin® Day Care Moisturizer. Great Skin is an honest-to-goodness skin care breakthrough. Because it contains a natural moisturizing complex of 12 ingredients called NMC-12.

NMC-12 is a unique formula which actually attracts moisture to the surface of your skin, like a sponge drawing up water. The moisture is drawn up from the natural reserves that lie deep within even the driest skin.

The remarkable effectiveness of Great Skin isn't just a theory. In repeated tests, hundreds of women found their skin to be smoother, dewier and more youthful—*in a matter of hours after use.*

You've tried other moisturizers, of course. But they can't do what Great Skin can do, because they don't have NMC-12. Try Great Skin, and soon your face will show the same youthful smoothness as the parts of your body that never show.

GREAT
SKIN
WITH
NMC-12
DAY CARE
MOISTURIZER
1 FL. OZ.

GREAT SKIN
Fabergé

Great Skin Day Care Moisturizer, Cleanser, Freshener, Night Care Cream, Hand Cream.

Fabergé Great Skin Lotion, 1976

I hate it, but I love it.

I figure anything that tastes that bad has got to work. And believe me, Listerine works! It even kills germs that can cause bad breath.

So sure I use it. Twice a day, in fact. And well... I haven't heard any complaints yet.

Listerine Antiseptic, 1971

She came on softly. There was something so silky about the way she looked. I wanted so much to get close to her. And as I did, she smelled so fresh, so real, so gentle.

JOHNSON's Baby Powder.
When a woman wants to make a gentle impression.

Johnson's Baby Powder, 1974

The Blemish Age: When you want to see her, but you make other plans.

"You can really think when you're alone. With my blemishes, I'll be a philosopher."

The blemish age. It's rough, but you can fight back. With Clearasil.

It's a special ointment with medicines that help dry up, heal acne blemishes. The same kind of medicines many dermatologists use. Because it's an ointment, Clearasil lets you concentrate its medicines directly on blemishes. And smoothing Clearasil on oily areas of your face helps drink up excess oil that you usually leave with blemishes.

Start now....wash your face thoroughly to get rid of surface dirt. Then apply Skin-Tone Clearasil to hide blemishes while it works, or White Vanishing that works invisibly. You fight blemishes and oil with either form of Clearasil, the most serious kind of acne medicine you can get without a prescription.

Clearasil, the serious blemish medicine.

Try Clearasil Medicated Soap. It's formulated to control surface skin bacteria and wash away excess oils. Clearasil Soap is as effective a medicated cleanser as you can buy today. And lots more economical.

Clearasil Blemish Medicine, 1971

Oh no!

The OH NO's—aggravating, frustrating acne blemishes that crop up at the worst possible times. Fight 'em with Clearasil. It contains the same ingredients many dermatologists use. Apply Clearasil all over your face. Double on stubborn OH NO's. And be smart. Help fight today's OH NO's, help prevent tomorrow's, by using Clearasil every day. It's the most serious kind of blemish medicine you can get without a prescription.

Clearasil. Oh yes.

Fight the OH NO's two ways!
(1) Skin-Tone Clearasil hides while it fights;
(2) White Vanishing Clearasil Cream Medication fights invisibly.

Clearasil Blemish Medicine, 1970

1. As a body softener for dry skin.
2. To moisturize your face.
3. In your bath to give your skin a natural glow.
4. To remove makeup.

5. As a hair conditioner to give your hair a healthy-looking sheen.
6. To massage tired muscles.
7. To help soften dry knees and elbows.

8. After diaper changes to clean and provide a protective moisture barrier.
9. To gently help remove cradle cap.
10. And to clean around ears.

© J&J 1976

How many ways can a family use *Johnson's* baby oil?

There are so many ways to feel a little softer, a little smoother with pure *Johnson's* baby oil, we haven't even discovered them all. But here are ten to start off with.

Johnson's baby oil

Johnson's Johnson

Johnson's Baby Oil, 1976

▶ *Psssssst Instant Shampoo, 1973*   ▶▶ *Kotex Sanitary Pads, 1970*

spray

fluff

brush

go!

Dear Mother Nature:

Drop dead!

Go on and say it. Then look at the brighter side. We're here.
Kotex® napkins with deep, downy Soft Impressions. The softer,
more absorbent kind that makes things easier for you. *Surer*.
And make darned sure you and Mother Nature hit it off. From
the start! Next time you start to get mad, remember us.

MR. BURNS
He's hot for your body.

Be prepared.
Take Unguentine® Aerosol.
It contains burn-chilling benzocaine
that lays a burst of cool on that sun pain.
Helps get Mr. Burns off your back.

Unguentine Aerosol
First-Aid for Sunburn.

Unguentine Sunburn Spray, 1974

▸ *d-CON Roach Traps,*

SPECIAL WINTER SALE!
LIMITED TIME ONLY
ONLY
$17⁹⁸
A WHOPPING 40% OFF
OUR REGULAR $29.98 PRICE!

NOW...WORLD'S FIRST LOW-COST IMPORTED FLAME GUN

Melts Ice Fast!...Burns Up Snow!

A fine buy at regular price—a give-away value at special super-sale price! You save $12! Never slip again—avoid dangerous falls—costly law suits! This quality jet-rod Flame Gun clears stairs, walks, driveways of even heaviest snow, thickest ice in seconds, frees "snowed in" cars. No heart-taxing shoveling—no bending. Easy, clean, one-hand operation from comfortable standing position. No cumbersome cords, no expensive batteries, no costly fuel!

SAFE...SIMPLE...COSTS MERE PENNIES PER USE!

In summer, kills weeds fast, sterilizes ground, gets rid of insect nests, keeps flagstone and cement walks clear, trims borders! Less than 2 pints of kerosene gives 30 minutes continuous use. Completely safe; weighs under 5 lbs; full instructions included. Order today—you will soon be paying $12 more! Next season, do your weeding without bending.

ONLY $17.98 plus $1.00 for postage and handling.
Prompt Shipment. Satisfaction Guaranteed. **HOBI**, Dept. IP-20 7 Delaware Drive, Lake Success, N.Y. 11040

MAIL NO-RISK COUPON TODAY

HOBI, Inc., Dept. IP-20
7 Delaware Drive, Lake Success, N.Y. 11040

Please rush ____ imported Flame Guns at special sale price of only $17.98 each plus $1.00 for postage and handling. If I am not absolutely delighted, I may return order for prompt refund, or full cancellation of charges any time within 10 days.
N.Y. residents, add sales tax.

☐ Check   ☐ Money Order for $ ____ enclosed.
☐ Charge my
☐ Diners Club #

(signature)

Name

Address

City ____ State ____ Zip ____

Flame Gun, 1970s

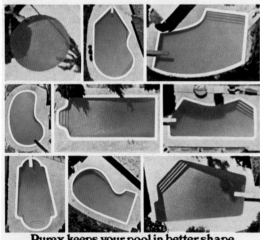

Purex keeps your pool in better shape no matter what shape your pool is in.

PUREX

Purex heaters, pumps, filters and underwater lights. **Guardex** quality chemicals, automatic chlorinators and test kits. Just ask your favorite pool builder, dealer or serviceman. Purex Corporation, Ltd., Pool Products Division

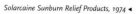

Solarcaine Sunburn Relief Products, 1974 ◄   *Purex Pool Supplies, 1973*

CUT OUT ALONG DOTTED LINE

3 BUCKS FOR A SMART BOY

VALUABLE COUPON WORTH $3 ON TANDY'S MODERN LEATHERCRAFT KIT

This coupon entitles you to receive Tandy's modern Leathercraft Kit for $10.95 (regularly priced $13.95). Just fill in and bring or mail this coupon to your nearest Tandy store listed below. Limit one coupon per person.
LS

Name

Address

City ____ State ____ Zip ____

Offer expires March 31, 1971. Good only at your Tandy store.
(If you order by mail don't forget to enclose $10.95 plus 75¢ postage)

Get America's Greatest Beginners' Leathercraft Kit at a Big $3 Savings.

Learn leathercraft while you are making leather articles for yourself, gifts or sale. Completed projects are worth more than the price of the kit. Kit has 8 projects to make of genuine leather. 8 Professional leather tools, lace, lacing needles, leather finishes, patterns, step by step picture instructions, manual, copy of "The Craftsman" Magazine.

Tandy's modern Leathercraft Kit will help earn your LEATHER WORK BADGE. The completed projects are worth more than the price of the entire kit.

Take or mail your coupon to the Tandy Leather store nearest you.

Regularly **$13.95**
WITH COUPON **$10.95**

Let's Do MODERN **LEATHERCRAFT**

Over 150 TANDY LEATHER Stores Coast to Coast.

Tandy's Leathercraft Kit, 1970   ► *Kohler Enclosure Habitat, 1979*

you can't live in a perfect climate. But that doesn't mean you can't own one.

Habitat,™ by Kohler.

Habitat is a remarkable addition to the series of Kohler environmental enclosures. It's designed to let you experience the soothing elements of warm Sun, refreshing Rain, and cleansing Steam, a delightful option. All within a single unit.

Habitat also gives you two conditioning elements, Ambience and Warm Breeze, to enhance the atmosphere. And warm the enclosure.

This is how it works. Select any element to begin your *Habitat* experience. When you're ready for a change, select another element ... or let *Habitat* sequence automatically every 20 minutes. You can also add conditioning elements as you wish. Add Warm Breeze to Sun, and you have a desert afternoon, buffed by light wind. Ambience and Rain create a bright summer shower.

The combinations seem endless. And so do the pleasures.

For all its uniqueness, *Habitat* is water and energy efficient. A one-hour sequence costs just about 25¢.

Habitat's suggested list price is about $5000, plus freight, installation, and options.

Learn more about *Habitat*. In the U.S. or Canada, look for your Kohler dealer in the Yellow Pages. Or send 50¢ to Kohler Co., Box AA, Kohler. WI 53044. *Habitat*, by Kohler. A climate you can own.

THE **BOLD LOOK** OF **KOHLER**

Occult Arts Society, 1974

"In this book I have read the age-abiding truths of the Scriptures with renewed interest and inspiration, as though coming to me direct from God. This paraphrase communicates the message of Christ to our generation. Your reading it will give you a new understanding of the Scriptures."
—Billy Graham

THE LIVING BIBLE PARAPHRASED

The greatest gift of all—the world's most readable Bible!

DOUBLEDAY

The Living Bible, 1971

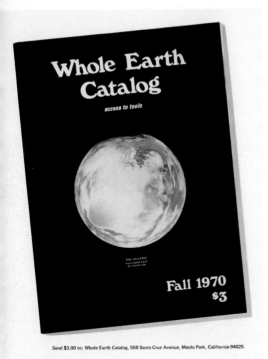

Apartment Life Posters, 1975 ◄   Whole Earth Catalog, 1970

WET Magazine, 1979   ► Poker Playing Dogs Posters, 1973

COOLIDGE'S FAMOUS SET OF POKER PLAYING DOGS
Our first time exclusive—Limited Edition in Color!

"A waterloo"

"Poker Sympathy"

"His Station & Four Aces"

"Pinched with Four Aces"

"A Friend in Need"
FREE!

Hurry! Poker buffs will snatch them up fast! Dog lovers will clean us out. Each picture a delight—so great is the artist's skill you can study it over and over and still discover new humor—additional detail.

The authentic original set of "Poker playing Dogs" by C. M. Coolidge—now in exclusive lithographs in full color. Each print is a large 12"x16", ready to frame—and our amazing buy enables us to sell them—not at $3 each—but at only $3 for the complete set of four—plus "A Friend in Need" (Publisher's list price $3) as a bonus, absolutely FREE of extra charge.

If you ever held 4 aces and still lost to a straight flush—if you ever played train poker and reached your station just as you got the hand of the year—you'll delight in "Poker Playing Dogs." Rush your $3 plus 25¢ postage and handling now to avoid disappointment. Or send only $5 for 2 sets and 2 FREE reprints of "A Friend in Need."

Sock it to him!

The versatile Banana Warmer.
One size fits all.
Give it to the man who has everything and no place to put it. It
holds and protects anything
from a banana and two
plums to the family jewels.
He can use it as a pipe
and tobacco pouch
or he can use his
imagination!

Swank Magazine Dept. SW-1, 50 W. 57th St., New York, N.Y. 10019
I know a man who fits the picture. I'd like to give him a Banana Warmer(s) and
enclose my check ☐ money order ☐ for $ ___
plus 50¢ postage and handling each. NYC. residents please add 8%
sales tax.

Name ___
Address ___
City ___
State ___
Zip ___

Viva Magazine, 1975 ◄ ◄   Penthouse Magazine, 1974 ◄

Swank Magazine Banana Warmer, 1975

Enter–
tainment
168

He runs it down the flagpole and up the establishment.

"PUTNEY SWOPE"

The Truth and Soul Movie

A Film by Robert Downey. A Cinema V Presentation.

SEE IT WHEN IT COMES TO A THEATRE NEAR YOU

Putney Swope, 1970

NORMAN MAILER, in *Armies of the Night*, calls Jerry Rubin "the most militant, unpredictable, creative — therefore dangerous — hippie-oriented leader available on the New Left."

DO IT!
Jerry Rubin

Introduction by
ELDRIDGE CLEAVER

In **DO IT!**, Jerry Rubin has written the most important political statement made by a white revolutionary in America today. It is *The Communist Manifesto* of our era and as a handbook for American revolutionaries must be compared to Che Guevara's *Guerrilla Warfare*.

DO IT! is a Declaration of War between the generations — calling on kids to raise a new society upon the ashes of the old.

DO IT! is a prose poem singing the inside saga of the movement; it is a frenzied emotional symphony for a new social disorder; a comic book for seven-year-olds; a tribute to insanity. Eldridge Cleaver has written an introduction to it and Quentin Fiore has designed the book with more than 100 pictures, cartoons and mind-zaps.

● Cloth: $5.95
Paper: $2.45

Simon and Schuster

Do It!, 1970

The Most Devastating Detective Story Of This Century.

REDFORD/HOFFMAN
"ALL THE PRESIDENT'S MEN"

Starring JACK WARDEN. Special appearance by MARTIN BALSAM. HAL HOLBROOK and JASON ROBARDS as Ben Bradlee
Screenplay by WILLIAM GOLDMAN • Based on the book by CARL BERNSTEIN and BOB WOODWARD • Music by DAVID SHIRE
Produced by WALTER COBLENZ • Directed by ALAN J. PAKULA
A Wildwood Enterprises Production • A Robert Redford-Alan J. Pakula Film

NOW PLAYING EVERYWHERE

Saturday Night Fever, 1977 ◄   *All the President's Men, 1976*

Premieres Christmas at selected theatres around the country.

Clint Eastwood
is Dirty Harry in
Magnum Force

Magnum Force, 1973   ► *Woodstock, 1970*

woodstock the movie

with a little help from our friends.)

starring   joan baez • joe cocker • country joe & the fish • crosby, stills, nash & young • arlo guthrie • richie havens • jimi hendrix
santana • john sebastian • sha-na-na • sly & the family stone • ten years after • the who • and 400,000 other beautiful people.

film by **michael wadleigh** • produced by bob maurice

a wadleigh-maurice, ltd. production • technicolor® from warner bros.

undtrack album on cotillion records and tapes

see it soon at a theatre near you

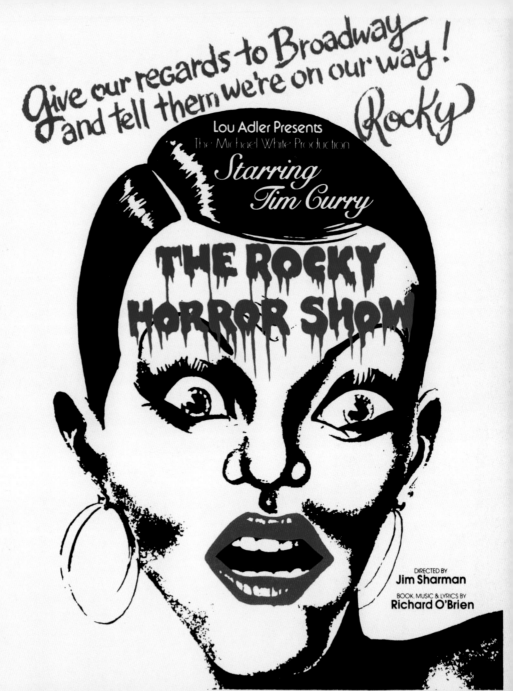

Give our regards to Broadway — and tell them we're on our way! (Rocky)

Lou Adler Presents
The Michael White Production
Starring
Tim Curry

THE ROCKY HORROR SHOW

DIRECTED BY
Jim Sharman

BOOK, MUSIC & LYRICS BY
Richard O'Brien

NEW YORK GRAND PREMIERE SUNDAY EVENING, MARCH 9 • SEATS NOW!
FRIDAY EVENING, MARCH 7 (Sold Out) 20TH CENTURY FOX PREVIEW—A SALUTE TO "ROCKY"
PUBLIC PREVIEW SATURDAY EVENING, MARCH 8 at 8 PM (Seats Available) $7.50, $6.5
REGULAR PRICES: Tues., Wed., Thurs. & Sun.—Orch. $11; Mezz. $8, 7, 6. Fri., Sat. & Opening Night—Orch. $13; Mezz. $10, 9, 8.
Please enclose stamped self-addressed envelope with check or money order and list alternate dates.   **AMERICAN EXPRESS ACCEPTED.**
REGULAR PERFORMANCE SCHEDULE: Tues., Wed. & Thurs. at 8 PM; 2 Perfs. Fri. & Sat. at 7:30 & 10:30 PM; Mat. Sun. at 3 PM.

THE BELASCO 44th St. East of B'way/JU 6-7950

jones is back and the devil's got him

the devil and mr. jones

X-RATED · COLOR
WORLD PREMIERE NOW · The BYRON · NEW YORK CITY
COMING SOON TO A THEATRE NEAR YOU.

The Rocky Horror Show, 1975 ◄

The Devil and Mr. Jones, 1975

"'THEY SHOOT HORSES, DON'T THEY?'

IS A MAGNIFICENT MOVIE: FORCEFUL, DIRECT, PROVOCATIVE, INVENTIVELY PRODUCED, SUPERBLY ACTED, HAUNT-
INGLY EFFECTIVE, IMMENSELY APPEALING AND TECHNICALLY BRILLIANT..."
—MICHAEL ROSS, LOS ANGELES HERALD-EXAMINER

"...DIRECTOR SYDNEY POLLACK, AN EX-ACTOR HIMSELF, DEVELOPS THE SIGNIFICANCE AND HANDLES THE CAST SO WELL,
SUBORDINATING AS IT SHOULD BE, THE FILM'S METAPHOR TO ACTION AND CHARACTER..."
—JOSEPH MORGENSTERN, NEWSWEEK

"... SYDNEY POLLACK, A BRILLIANT YOUNG DIRECTOR-ARTIST, PROVES HIMSELF A MASTER OF THE BIG SCREEN WITH
'HORSES'. IN CAPTURING A TIME AND PLACE ALIEN TO HIM, HE SHOWS IN THIS HIGHLY PERSONAL DIRECTORIAL VISION
WHAT A FILM CAN BE IN THE HANDS OF ONE WHO UNDERSTANDS IT..."
—JOYCE HABER, TIMES-MIRROR SYNDICATE

"... 'HORSES' SHOULD GARNER AN OSCAR NOMINATION FOR DIRECTOR SYDNEY POLLACK..."
—DOROTHY MANNERS, KING FEATURES

They Shoot Horses, Don't They?, 1970

Director Mark Rydell creates dazzling images – moves with rhythm and style, ROLAND
GELATT, SATURDAY REVIEW - "The Reivers," which was artistically and sensitively directed
by Mark Rydell, may be added to that classic list such as "Shane." It is that good,
RONA BARRETT, METROMEDIA - It would take space four times this long to detail all
the things I liked about Mark Rydell's direction. MARY KNOBLAUCH, CHICAGO TODAY -
Director Mark Rydell has artfully captured the flavor of the period, deftly balanced the mood
and language of Faulkner, and has drawn memorable performances out of his cast, BOB
PORTER, DALLAS TIMES HERALD - Director Mark Rydell has put "The Reivers" on film with
devotion and total respect. There are beautiful scenes which he has managed with real
understanding, ALTA MALONEY, BOSTON HERALD TRAVELER - Rydell's direction is straight-
forward and imaginative. He draws exquisitely balanced performances from his three stars,
SUSAN STARK, DETROIT FREE PRESS - Mark Rydell, a brilliant young director-artist, proves
himself a master of the big screen with "The Reivers," JOYCE HABER.

"The Reivers"

An Irving Ravetch-Arthur Kramer Production —
In Association with Solar Productions
A Cinema Center Films Presentation
A National General Pictures Release

The Reivers, 1970

"What kind of people are you?"

"Hardy Kruger's support
is a tour de force...
He dominates every scene
he is in."
—HANK GRANT, HOLLYWOOD REPORTER

STANLEY KRAMER'S Production of
"THE SECRET OF SANTA VITTORIA"
United Artists

The Secret of Santa Vittoria, 1970

"The squeamish, the weak-
hearted, or the simply
tender-hearted are quite
seriously warned away.
Those who go will see a brilliantly made, thought-
provoking movie!"
Charles Champlin,
L.A. TIMES

"... A raucous, violent, magnificent, powerful feat of
American film making ...
extraordinarily forceful
acting!"
TIME MAGAZINE

"...'Wild Bunch' will justify
almost any superlatives you
want to apply to it ... one of
4 best pictures of the year!"
Winfred Blevins,
L.A. HERALD-EXAMINER

THE WILD BUNCH

Special Screening for Academy Members of the following branches:
Executive & Administrators / January 26
Producers / January 27
Short Subjects / January 28

Each night at 8:30 P.M. Warner Bros. Studio (North Gate) Warner Boulevard

The Wild Bunch, 1970   ▶ *Midnight Cowboy, 1970*

Dustin Hoffman gives one of the screen's more incredible and powerful performances." —FORT WORTH STAR-TELEGRAM

"MIDNIGHT COWBOY"   A JEROME HELLMAN-JOHN SCHLESINGER PRODUCTION

The Rose, 1979

Liquid Space, 1974

TED KRAMER IS ABOUT TO LEARN WHAT 10 MILLION WOMEN ALREADY KNOW.

He's got a wife he wants to get back, and a kid he won't ever let go.
His boy is teaching him how to make French toast, the girl in the office

wants to sleep over, and he has to juggle his job and the PTA.
For Ted Kramer, life is going to be full of surprises.

Columbia Pictures presents a Stanley Jaffe production

Dustin Hoffman
in
"Kramer vs. Kramer"
Meryl Streep Jane Alexander

Director of Photography Nestor Almendros Based upon the novel by Avery Corman Produced by Stanley R. Jaffe
Written for the screen and directed by Robert Benton

© 1979 COLUMBIA PICTURES INDUSTRIES INC

Opens December 19th at selected theatres.

"THRILLING BOTH AS TO FACT AND IN THE FILM'S RECOUNTING OF IT! THE RAW TRUTH BOGGLES THE MIND AND OUT PACES THE IMAGINATION! Al Pacino provides one of the outstanding performances of the year!" —Judith Crist

A PARAMOUNT RELEASE
DINO DE LAURENTIIS
presents

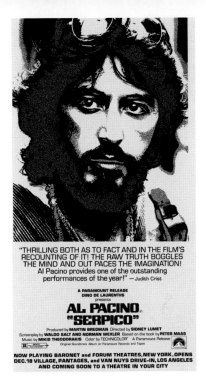

AL PACINO in
"SERPICO"

Produced by MARTIN BREGMAN Directed by SIDNEY LUMET
Screenplay by WALDO SALT AND NORMAN WEXLER Based on the book by PETER MAAS
Music by MIKIS THEODORAKIS Color by TECHNICOLOR A Paramount Release
Original Soundtrack Album on Paramount Records and Tapes

NOW PLAYING BARONET and FORUM THEATRES, NEW YORK, OPENS DEC. 18 VILLAGE, PANTAGES, and VAN NUYS DRIVE-IN, LOS ANGELES AND COMING SOON TO A THEATRE IN YOUR CITY

Kramer vs. Kramer, 1979

Serpico, 1974

A STAR IS BORN

The original sound track music from the Warner Bros. film starring Barbra Streisand and Kris Kristofferson. The movie will be released to theatres nationwide at Christmas. The album is available now on Columbia Records and Tapes.

Now a paperback from Warner Books

Album produced by: Barbra Streisand and Phil Ramone.

Available at

IT'S "A SMASH"! (—New York Times) IT'S "HILARIOUS" (—Gannett Newspapers) IT'S ★★★★ (—New York Daily News) IT'S "ONE OF THE GREAT AMERICAN MOVIES"! (—New York Magazine) IT'S "MAGNIFICENT"! (—Saturday Review) IT'S "AN ORGY FOR MOVIE LOVERS"! (—New Yorker Magazine) IT'S "A WINNER"! (—Metromedia TV) IT'S "A BLOCKBUSTER"! (—After Dark Playboy) IT'S "BRILLIANTLY ORIGINAL"! (—Family Circle) IT'S THE DAMNDEST THING YOU EVER SAW!

NASHVILLE

RESTRICTED

——EXCLUSIVE NORTHERN CALIFORNIA ENGAGEMENT——

NORTHPOINT
POWELL & BAY · 989-6060

NOW SHOWING

MATINEES DAILY — Shows Daily At: 2:00, 4:45, 7:30 And 10:00 P.M.
ADJACENT FREE PARKING AFTER 6PM & ALL DAY SUN. AND HOLIDAYS.

70

That's Entertainment, 1974 ◄

A Star Is Born, 1976

Nashville, 1975

"We can do anything we want.
We're college students!"

NATIONAL LAMPOON's

ANIMAL HOUSE

A comedy from Universal Pictures that will escape sometime this summer.

Starring: John Belushi, Tim Matheson, John Vernon, Verna Bloom, Thomas Hulce,
and Donald Sutherland as "Jennings"

Plus a cast of 4,623 other very funny people.

Produced by Matty Simmons and Ivan Reitman
Directed by John Landis
Written by Harold Ramis, Doug Kenney, and Chris Miller

National Lampoon's Animal House, 1978

▶ *Apocalypse Now, 1979*

FRANCIS FORD COPPOLA
PRESENTS

Apocalypse Now

MARLON BRANDO   ROBERT DUVALL   MARTIN SHEEN in APOCALYPSE NOW
FREDERIC FORREST ALBERT HALL SAM BOTTOMS LARRY FISHBURNE and DENNIS HOPPER
Produced and Directed by FRANCIS COPPOLA
Written by JOHN MILIUS and FRANCIS COPPOLA
Co-Produced by FRED ROOS, GRAY FREDERICKSON and TOM STERNBERG
Director of Photography VITTORIO STORARO Production Designer DEAN TAVOULARIS Editor RICHARD MARKS
Sound Design by WALTER MURCH Music by CARMINE COPPOLA and FRANCIS COPPOLA

WORLD PREMIERE AUGUST 15th AT THE CINERAMA DOME THEATRE
Reserved tickets now on sale at box office or by mail.

Andy Warhol's

FRANKENSTEIN

A Film by
Paul Morrissey
in

3D

RATED
X

NO ONE UNDER 17 ADMITTED

ANDY WARHOL'S "FRANKENSTEIN" · A Film by PAUL MORRISSEY · Starring Joe Dallesandro
Monique Van Vooren · Udo Kier · Introducing Arno Juerging · Dalila Di Lazzaro · Srdjan Zelenovic
A CARLO PONTI – BRAUNSBERG – RASSAM PRODUCTION 🎬 COLOR · A BRYANSTON PICTURES RELEASE

Andy Warhol's Frankenstein, 1974

▶ *Revenge of the Pink Panther, 1978*

PETER SELLERS in
BLAKE EDWARDS'

REVENGE
OF THE
PINK
PANTHER

© UAC- 1978

Starring HERBERT LOM · ROBERT WEBBER
with DYAN CANNON
Music HENRY MANCINI — Executive Producer TONY ADAMS
Screen Play by FRANK WALDMAN · RON CLARK · BLAKE EDWARDS
Animation DePATIE · FRELENG
tory by BLAKE EDWARDS — Produced and Directed by BLAKE EDWARDS

 United Artists
A Transamerica Company

STAR TREK
THE MOTION PICTURE ™

THE HUMAN ADVENTURE IS JUST BEGINNING.

Paramount Pictures Presents A GENE RODDENBERRY Production A ROBERT WISE Film STAR TREK—THE MOTION PICTURE Starring WILLIAM SHATNER LEONARD NIMOY DeFOREST KEL
Co-Starring JAMES DOOHAN GEORGE TAKEI MAJEL BARRETT WALTER KOENIG NICHELLE NICHOLS Presenting PERSIS KHAMBATTA and Starring STEPHEN COLLINS as Decker Music by JERR
Screenplay by HAROLD LIVINGSTON Story by ALAN DEAN FOSTER Produced by GENE RODDENBERRY Directed by ROBERT WISE A Paramount Picture

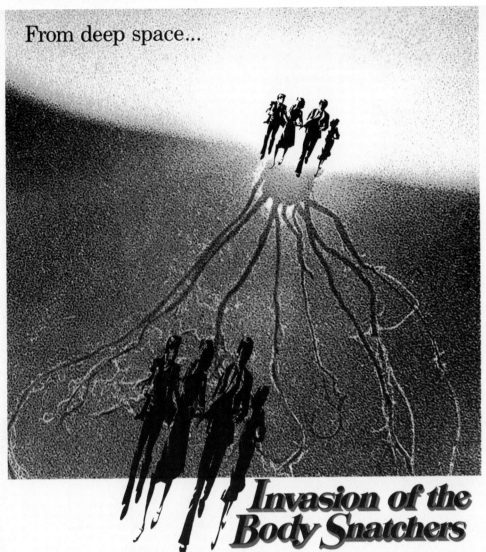

From deep space...

Invasion of the Body Snatchers

The seed is planted...terror grows.

A Robert H. Solo Production of A Philip Kaufman Film
"Invasion of the Body Snatchers"
Donald Sutherland · Brooke Adams · Leonard Nimoy
Jeff Goldblum · Veronica Cartwright · Screenplay by W. D. Richter,
Based on the novel "The Body Snatchers" by Jack Finney · Produced by Robert H. Solo

DOLBY STEREO ™ Directed by Philip Kaufman ☰ United Artists A Transamerica Company PG PARENTAL GUIDANCE SUGGESTED SOME MATERIAL MAY NOT BE SUITABLE FOR CHILDREN

STARTS DECEMBER 22ND AT SPECIALLY SELECTED THEATERS!

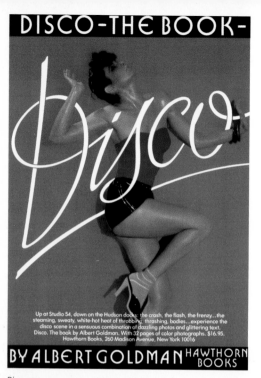

Disco, 1979

Thank God It's Friday, 1978

Adam & Yves, 1972

▶ *Swept Away...*, 1975   ▶▶ *Fillmore*, 1972

"Swept Away..."

A film by Lina Wertmuller

Clay Theatre

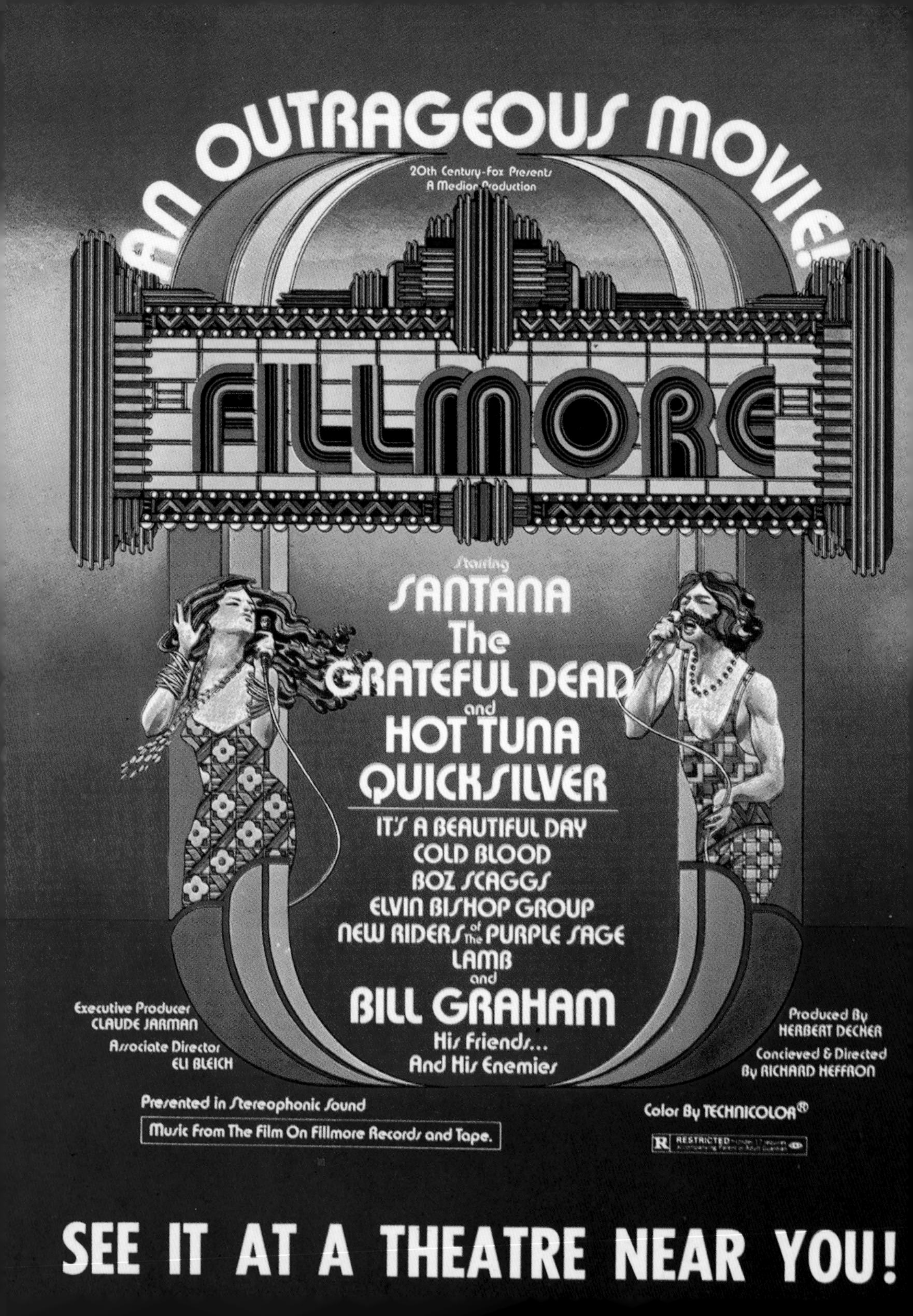

AN OUTRAGEOUS MOVIE!

20th Century-Fox Presents
A Medion Production

FILLMORE

Starring

SANTANA
The GRATEFUL DEAD
and
HOT TUNA
QUICKSILVER

IT'S A BEAUTIFUL DAY
COLD BLOOD
BOZ SCAGGS
ELVIN BISHOP GROUP
NEW RIDERS of The PURPLE SAGE
LAMB
and
BILL GRAHAM
His Friends...
And His Enemies

Executive Producer
CLAUDE JARMAN

Associate Director
ELI BLEICH

Produced By
HERBERT DECKER

Concieved & Directed
By RICHARD HEFFRON

Presented in Stereophonic Sound

Music From The Film On Fillmore Records and Tape.

Color By TECHNICOLOR®

SEE IT AT A THEATRE NEAR YOU!

PARAMOUNT PICTURES PRESENTS

The Godfather PART II

Michael's family album

Original motion picture soundtrack recording.

 Records

KSAN FM 95
A METROMEDIA STEREO STATION
SAN FRANCISCO
robert otis holter

The Godfather: Part II Soundtrack, 1975 ◄◄   *KSAN Radio Station, 1976* ◄

KSAN Radio Station, 1975

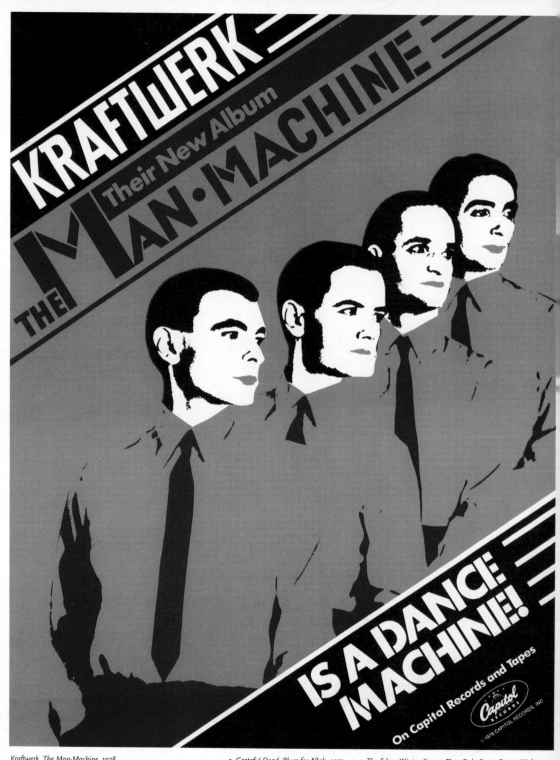

Kraftwerk, *The Man-Machine*, 1978

▶ *Grateful Dead, Blues for Allah, 1975* ▶ ▶ *The Edgar Winter Group, They Only Come Out at Night, 1973*

proudly present
"Blues For Allah".
A brilliant musical achievement
from the legendary
Grateful Dead.

Listen To This Ad.

John Lennon
Walls and Bridges

SW-3416

apple records
from Capitol Records

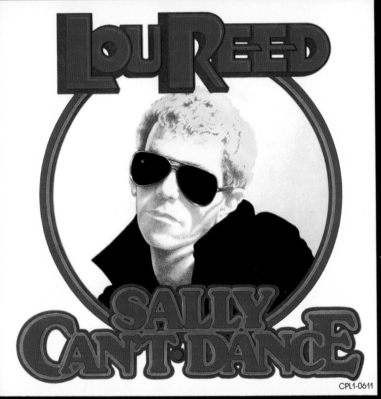

earotic.

CPL1-0611

His new album.
The way rock was <u>meant</u> to roll.

Produced by Steve Katz and Lou Reed

RCA Records and Tapes

John Lennon, Walls and Bridges, 1974 ◀◀   Cher, Take Me Home, 1979 ◀   Lou Reed, Sally Can't Dance, 1974   ▶ The Village People, Cruisin', 1978

197

If You Think "Macho Man" Is Hot, Wait Till You Start

Cruisin'

The Hot New LP From The Dynamic

VILLAGE PEOPLE

on Casablanca Record and FilmWorks

Composed and Produced by JACQUES MORALI for CAN'T STOP PRODUCTIONS, INC Executive Producer: HENRI BELOLO

Linda Ronstadt, Silk Purse, 1970

Bette Midler, The Divine Miss M, 1973

Bob Marley & The Wailers, 1976 ◄   Rita Coolidge, The Lady's Not For Sale, 1973

Joni Mitchell, Court and Spark, 1974   ► Bongo Fury, 1975

ZAPPA / BEEFHEART
MOTHERS
BONGO FURY
LIVE IN CONCERT AT ARMADILLO WORLD HEADQUARTERS
AUSTIN, TEXAS
May 20th & 21st, 1975

ON THE BEACH
NEIL YOUNG

WALK ON · SEE THE SKY ABOUT TO RAIN · REVOLUTION BLUES · FOR THE TURNSTILES · VAMPIRE BLUES · ON THE BEACH · MOTION PICTURES · AMBULANCE BLUES

Neil Young, On the Beach, 1974

▶ *Cat Stevens, Foreigner, 1973*

Supertramp, Breakfast is Served, 1979

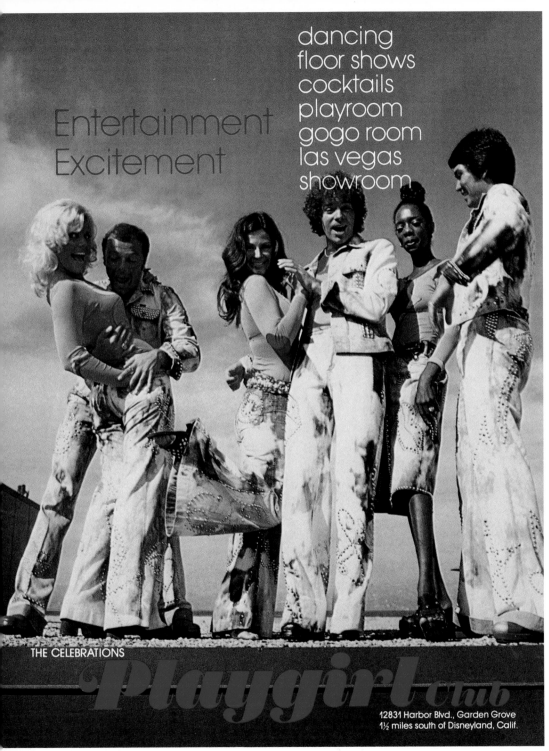

Entertainment
Excitement

dancing
floor shows
cocktails
playroom
gogo room
las vegas
showroom

THE CELEBRATIONS

Playgirl club

12831 Harbor Blvd., Garden Grove
1½ miles south of Disneyland, Calif.

Playgirl Club, 1974

Fashion & Beauty
206

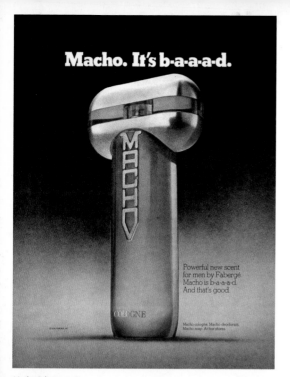

Macho Cologne, 1976

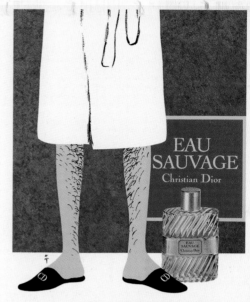

Eau Sauvage Cologne, 1977

After Six Accessories, 1972 ◄

Ginseng Cologne, 1976

English Leather Cologne, 1979

► *Jovan Sex Appeal After Shave, 1978*

Now that you have acquired the power my son, you must swear to me by the sacred sword of Jōvan, that you will use the power only for good... never for evil.

CHAZ

The fragrance that's almost as interesting as the men who wea

BRYLCREEM SAYS DON'T MEASURE YOUR SEX APPEAL BY THE LENGTH OF YOUR HAIR.

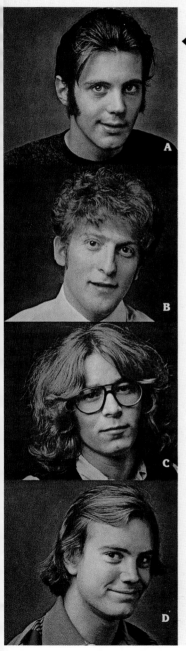

← NOT SEXY   SEXY →

A. Sideburns too long and too wide. End result: not too terrific. We said goodbye to sideburns and let his hair grow 1½ inches all over. Then gave it a layered cut.

Also recommended: frequent shampooing with Brylcreem Once A Day Shampoo to condition the hair while washing away excess oil, dirt and loose dandruff.

B. This guy was fighting natural curl with a cut that was too closely cropped on sides and back. We let it grow for two months and shaped it.

Because curly hair is porous and tends to dry out quickly, we used a dab of Brylcreem to condition while helping to keep the hair neat and manageable all day.

C. Too much hair, too little face. We took off 5 inches. Gave him a scissor cut, parted on the side to add more width and fullness to the top.

When hair goes through this change from very long to short, it needs about a week to lay right. Help it along with Brylcreem Power Hold, a specially formulated control hair spray that provides real holding power all day.

D. This guy's hair was all wrong for the shape of his face. Too long in back and too much of one length.

We cut off 2½ inches in front, 3 inches in back. We layered it on top for more body and gave him a geometric cut along the edges for the New Short look.

Brylcreem believes that sexy is as sexy does. And when your hair really does something for you, then you've got sex appeal.

The Brylcreem group.

We've come a long way since "a little dab'll do ya."

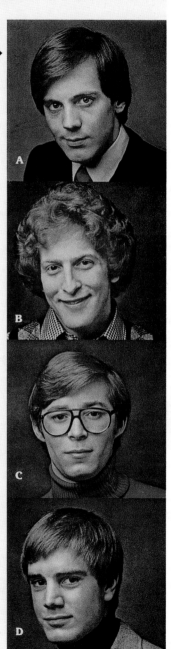

Chaz Cologne, 1979 ◄

Brylcreem Men's Hair Product, 1974

Kama mama, kama binti
(Like mother, like daughter)

Kama mama, kama binti is poetry in Swahili. And your little girl's
natural is proud poetry in velvety rings and curls.
Such beauty deserves the same loving care as your own crowning
glory. Naturally, we mean Afro Sheen® concentrated shampoo
and Afro Sheen® conditioner & hair dress. The best for both of you.

wantu wazuri use afro sheen®

 JOHNSON PRODUCTS CO., INC., CHICAGO, ILLINOIS 60620

ULTRA NATURAL

Maybe you've wanted to go natural but put it off because you thought your hair could only look one way.

Well, you don't have to wait any more. You can wear an Ultra Natural.

After your beautician relaxes your hair with Ultra Sheen Permanent Creme Relaxer she sets it with special large-size rollers.

When the comb it out, you have a beautiful new kind of natural. The Ultra Natural. With an ultra soft, ultra feminine look.

And if you should ever decide to change your hairstyle, just wash and reset your hair with Ultra Sheen Rinse 'N' Set. You can be ultra curly, ultra smooth, anything you want.

That's one more beautiful thing about the Ultra Natural. Its natural only when you want it to be.

Be a natural woman. Relax. With Ultra Sheen Permanent Creme Relaxer.

Ultra Sheen Relaxer, 1970

Who can say "no" to a gorgeous brunette?

Black can be as beautiful as you make it... if you make it happen with the magic of Loving Care.® It's the gentle haircoloring. Washes away the gray while it enriches your natural hair color.

It's different. Nothing to mix. No peroxide, so it can't really change your natural shade.

Easy to do, too. It's a lotion. Just pour it on. Even has its own wonderful conditioner to keep your hair shiny.

So you can be as beautifully black on the outside as you are on the inside.

And you can't get any more natural than that.

Loving Care®—the gentle hair color from Clairol for natural, pressed and relaxed hair.

Clairol Loving Care Hair Color, 1970

"I have a terrific new way to wash my hair. It's a shampoo with vitamins, minerals, protein and herbs."

"I have a new formula for livelier, shinier, healthier-looking hair. Farrah Fawcett Shampoo. Fabergé created it, and put in good things I believe in—things hair has naturally: vitamins, minerals and keratin, hair's own protein.

Plus garden herbs to leave your hair delicious-smelling. And soft cleansers—as gentle as the ones in fine complexion soaps—so you can shampoo as often as you shower.

Try Farrah Fawcett Shampoo. And my new Creme Rinse/Conditioner and Hair Spray, too. I'm sure you'll find something beautiful happens to your hair."

Fabergé introduces Farrah

Fawcett Hair Care

Something beautiful happens to your hair.

Afro Sheen Hair Products, 1971 ◄   *Farrah Fawcett Hair Care, 1978*

► *"Gee, Your Hair Smells Terrific" Shampoo, 1975*

Gee, your hair smells terrific! Like no other fragrance around. Slightly flowery. Slightly spicy. Deliciously nice to be near.

It looks terrific, too. Clean. Soft. Full of bounce and sunshine.

New, "Gee, Your Hair Smells Terrific." Fragrance shampoo that's gentle as a whisper. And same-fragrance, rich-rich conditioner. Try them both.

"GEE,YOUR HAIR SMELLS TERRIFIC."
Shampoo & conditioner with fragrance that goes to your head. And to his!

©1972 Clairol, Inc.

Now there's a velvet *creme rinse* to follow the beautiful Clairol® herbal essence shampoo experience.
It makes your hair so fresh and tame and luscious, you'll think you're handling flower petals.

Introducing Clairol® herbal essence Creme Rinse.

Inside Clairol's beautiful new creme rinse is the breathtakingly fresh essence of mysterious green herbs and enchanted flowers. Like Melissa. Mountain Gentian. Juniper. And birch leaves. The same beautiful combination of earthy pleasures that makes the famous Clairol herbal essence shampoo such a beautiful experience.

Besides the wildly fresh way new Clairol herbal essence creme rinse makes your hair smell, it also gives your hair the velvety soft texture of the inside of a rose petal. And helps it to comb like silk right down to the ends. Treat your hair to the newest pleasure from the garden of earthly delights. The beautiful new Clairol herbal essence creme rinse.

Glow
for the
Holidays

To keep your looks as sparkling bright as the
holiday season ahead, turn up your glow to a holiday intensity.
Glisten your lips, your eyes, and your cheeks with Posner
Custom Blends Cosmetics.
Posner Custom Blends won't fade, won't change
color. They're especially formulated to be low-in-oils and
right-in-color, so they stay fresh
and natural all day long. Look for
Posner Custom Blends Cosmetics
at your favorite cosmetics counter
or write: Posner Laboratories, Inc.,
Corona, N.Y. 11368.

POSNER
CUSTOM BLENDS
COSMETICS

Posner Custom Blends Cosmetics, 1974

**"GEE, YOUR HAIR
SMELLS TERRIFIC!"**

"Gee, Your Hair Smells Terrific" is
the shampoo made to leave hair
smelling terrific. With a soft, young
breezy-fresh fragrance. Like
meadows of wildflowers in spring.
But that's not all. "Gee" makes hair
feel super-clean, too! Leaves it
soft, silky and very shiny. Because
isn't that why you wash your hair
in the first place? "Gee, Your
Hair Smells Terrific" Shampoo and
same-fragrance Conditioner. Try them
both and see: they're terrific!

**FRAGRANCE SHAMPOO &
FRAGRANCE CONDITIONER.**
Available in normal/dry and oily hair formulas.

"Gee, Your Hair Smells Terrific" Shampoo, 1979

The frost that's a lipstick.
The frost that's a lip conditioner.
The frost that's a lipgloss.

Revlon creates Frost Formula 2.

The only lipfrost and lipgloss in one.
Colors. Conditions. Shines.

Frost Formula 2.
Now. From the Revlon Research Group.

Clairol Herbal Essence Creme Rinse, 1973 ◄ *Revlon Lipstick, 1972*

► *Royal Shield Hair Products, 1972*

Posner Custom Blends Cosmetics, 1971

Posner Custom Blends Cosmetics, 1972 ◄   CornSilk Cosmetics, 1974   Fabergé Cosmetics, 1974   ► Chanel No. 5 Perfume, 1977

219

The Clinique Computer will see you now.

It will be a revelation.

In a quick 30-second consultation, you will learn your skin type, you will learn how to have better and better looking skin. Developed by a group of leading dermatologists, the fast, informative Clinique Computer Analysis is available at no charge at any Clinique Counter.

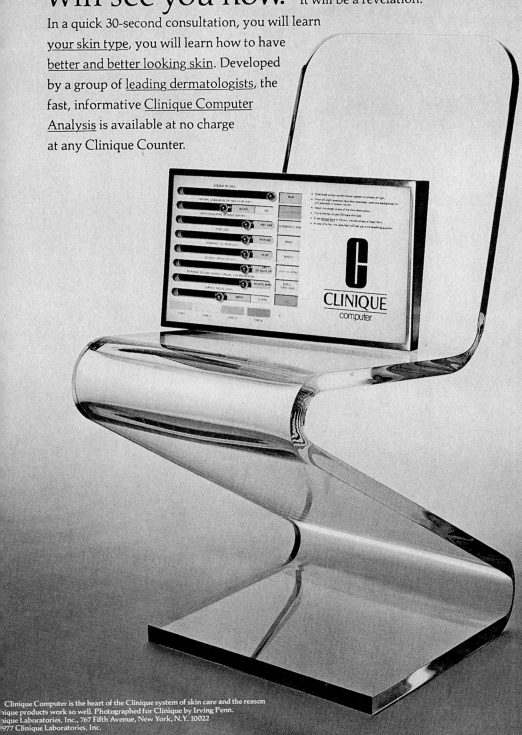

Hot Pants Slenderizer, 1971

Sauna Belt Waistline Reducer, 1970

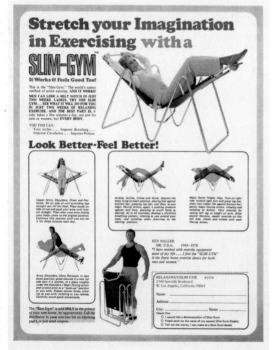

Clinique Cosmetics, 1977 ◄

Slim-Gym Exerciser, 1970

Trim-Jeans Slenderizer, 1971

► *Levi's, 1971*

Levi's, 1970

Landlubber Clothes, 1971

Enka, 1974

Mr. Hicks Casuals, 1971 ▸ Padrino Fashions, 1974

a
whole
new way
of
walking

PADRINO

marshmallows, platforms and down to earth fashions

ERLING IMPORTS, INC. 350 Fifth Avenue (Suite 7419) New York, N.Y. 10001

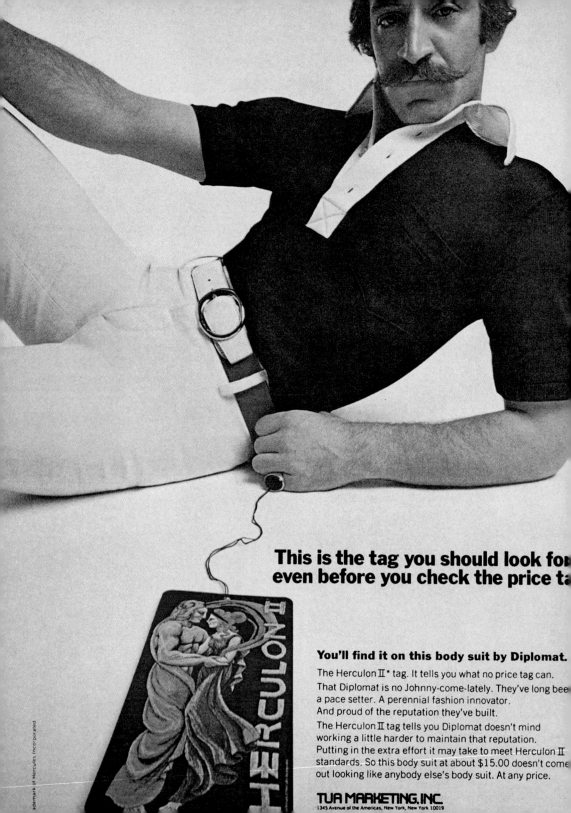

**This is the tag you should look for
even before you check the price ta**

You'll find it on this body suit by Diplomat.

The Herculon II* tag. It tells you what no price tag can.

That Diplomat is no Johnny-come-lately. They've long bee
a pace setter. A perennial fashion innovator.
And proud of the reputation they've built.

The Herculon II tag tells you Diplomat doesn't mind
working a little harder to maintain that reputation.
Putting in the extra effort it may take to meet Herculon II
standards. So this body suit at about $15.00 doesn't come
out looking like anybody else's body suit. At any price.

TUA MARKETING, INC.
1345 Avenue of the Americas, New York, New York 10019

Above all...Phoenix Clothes

Phoenix Clothes, 1974

Encron Strialine Polyester, 1976

Geoffrey Beene Men's Wear, 1974

Enkalure Nylon, 1975

London Fog Trench Coats, 1972

▶ *Rainfair Trench Coats, 1975*

he Acapulco

eling people select this single
sted trench coat of 100%
ron® polyester for its tra-
nal styling features and
pile zip-out liner. A
ion winner from our
ners Circle collec-
of rain-topcoats.
ont ZEPEL® pro-
ed against rain
ain. About $87.50.
ks by Smartair.

A Koracorp Company

Rainfair

DUPONT
ZEPEL
RAIN / STAIN REPELLER

flagg Bros.

Men's Fashions By Mail

Walk proud in the MELLOW MOVER. A smooth black and burgundy leather lace-up. Newest tap sole and all-leather maxi heel. Biscuit toe. Curving leather accents around eyelets and toe. Style #6018. Only $17.99 by mail.

Be a cool stepper in the SOUL STRUTTER. A bold tan and black leather wingtip lace-up. Covered platform sole. Flared maxi heel. Style #6104. Only $16.99 by mail.

#6018

#6104

#S546

Put on non-stop style with the pucker knit shirt of acetate and nylon. Handsome 8-inch long point collar and cool balloon sleeves. Black #S540, Wine #S541, Royal Blue #S546. Only $12.99 by mail.

#S587

Get it on in this soulful shirt of luxurious Dacron and Rayon. Crocheted edging accents the 7-inch long point collar and front closing. Black #S580, Brown #S585, Yellow #S587. Only $15.99 by mail.

Walk tall in these 30-inch flare bottom slacks. Styled with 2 button extension waistband, western front and back flap pockets. Black #P140, Burgundy #P141, Gray #P142, Gold #P147. Waist sizes 27-34, 36, 38. Only $17.99 by mail.

#1778

The only way to go is up with the RILL THING. A smooth red and black leather lace-up. Bold red leather piping, platform sole and covered maxi-heel. Style #1778. Only $17.99 by mail.

#A811

Be your own kind of man in the DO-THE-DO toga suit. Coat and slacks are styled from luxurious acetate and nylon. Tunic is trimmed in imitation Persian lamb. Slacks feature 22-inch flare bottoms and extended waistband. Black #A810, Beige #A814, Burgundy #811. Coat Sizes S, M, L, XL. Waist sizes 28, 30, 32, 34, 36, 38. Only $42.99 by mail.

#P140

Cut along dotted line.

send for all new free catalog

Check here for FREE CATALOG ☐

NAME _____ ADDRESS _____
(please print)   street
CITY _____ STATE _____ ZIP _____

If you are ordering any item from this page, fill in the following form.
Shoes in D widths only. Order slacks by waist size. Slacks shipped with unfinished bottoms. Shirt sizes S (14-14½) M (15-15½) L (16-16½) XL (17-17½)

STYLE # _____ SIZE _____ STYLE # _____ SIZE _____
STYLE # _____ SIZE _____ STYLE # _____ SIZE _____

(If money order, add $1.25 uniform postage fees and insurance. For C.O.D., add $1 deposit. No C.O.D.'s can be delivered to A.P.O. or F.P.O., or any foreign country. Orders to these addresses must be paid in advance. Tennessee residents, add 5% sales tax.) ☐ Money Order ☐ C.O.D.

Send to: **flagg Bros.** Dept. E-11 492 Craighead St., Nashville, Tennessee 37204

Flagg Bros. has these and many other man-making styles in their FREE full color catalog.

Johnny Carson Apparel, 1974 ◄ *Flagg Bros. Men's Fashions, 1974*

▶ *Adam Briefs, 1976*

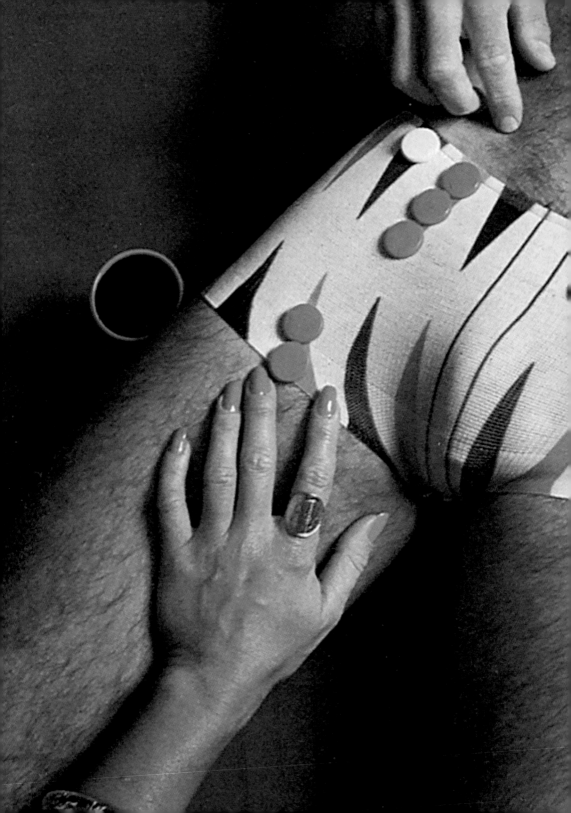

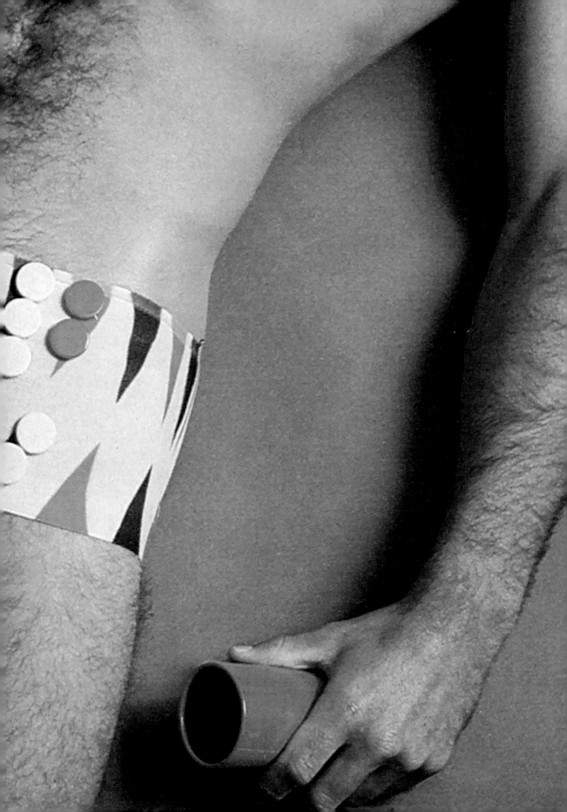

SOFTMAGIC™
with reinforced panty/toe,
also in sheer-to-the-waist
and outsize. From $1.19*

PANTI-PANTYHOSE™
with cotton crotch, also in
control top and outsize.
From $1.49*

Assorted Fruit
Pantyhose from 99¢

BUDGETEER™
sheer-to-the-waist, also
with reinforced
panty/toe, 99¢*

GREAT SHAPE™
control top with sandal
foot, $1.99*. Also with
reinforced toe.
Outsize, $1.79
(not shown)

GREAT SHAPE™
sheer support, $2.99*

*Whatever style fits your style,
you'll feel sheer, comfortable, confident.
And Assorted Fruit of the Loom
prices from 99¢* fit nicely in a budget
for a busy lifestyle, too.
Ask for them at
your favorite store.*

FRUIT OF THE LOOM.
UNCONDITIONALLY GUARANTEED

Manufacturer's suggested retail price.   Manufactured under license from Fruit of the Loom, Inc. • New York, NY

Fruit of the Loom Panty Hose, 1978

► *Interwoven Socks, 1972*

Announcing the best-dressed men in America.

You're looking at a revolution.
The most influential men in America are breaking out of their socks—out of their old, blah, boring, one-color, no-style socks.
At Interwoven/Esquire Socks, we saw it coming all the way. That's why we make the great fashion socks that are making it happen.
In lots of great colors and lengths. All in the first

Ban-Lon® pattern socks ever made. They feel softer and fit better than any sock you've ever worn.
That's why we dress the best-dressed men in America. Or anywhere.

Peter Max paints panty hose for Burlington-Cameo.

they come in three proportioned-to-fit sizes, $8.00 each. body stockings, too. one size only, in 2 peter max original designs (not shown). cost $10.00 each. buy the panty hose or body stockings and you get a coupon for a peter max poster. (it's a copy of this page blown up to poster size 24″x36″.) send us the coupon you'll find in the package and one dollar to cover handling and postage. we'll send you the poster. who knows, your room might even look as good as your legs.

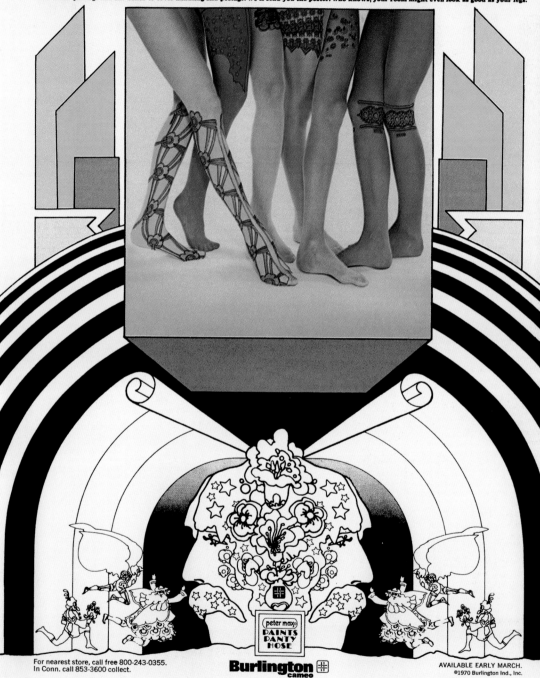

For nearest store, call free 800-243-0355.
In Conn. call 853-3600 collect.

Burlington cameo

AVAILABLE EARLY MARCH.
©1970 Burlington Ind., Inc.

Burlington Panty Hose, 1972

Big Mama,

you're beautiful.
(You're even guaranteed for 30-days-wear-or-a-new-pair.)

Beautifully fitting and sheer, from top to toe, be you Large or Extra Large* Big Mama pantyhose—thanks to your new Captiva® nylon yarn's super stretch, strength and wearability.

Beautifully long-wearing, as evidenced by your guarantee of 30 days wear or a new pair, no matter what.

Beautifully practical with your exclusive reusable panty.

Beautifully comfortable, with not a single lump, bump, bulge, seam, or wrinkle to be seen or felt.

Beautifully beautiful in your fifteen luscious sheer shades.

And beautifully economical*, at Ardens Shops, Gemco, Memco, Wonderworld and other fine chain, drug and variety stores everywhere. Or, write: Sheffield Hosiery Mills, 1190 N.W. 159th Drive, Miami, Florida 33169. A division of Sheffield Industries, Inc.

Captiva. They last.
nylon

*TRADE MARK   ALLIED CHEMICAL CORPORATION   Allied Chemical

*Large: 5'-5'9", 165-230 lbs. Extra Large: 5'-5'9", 230-260 lbs. Sunlight, beige-tone, tantone, taupetone, cinnamon, twilite, coffee, navy, off-white, off-black, white in all styles. Plus plum, red onion, rust and grey in Large Big Mama only. Large, Extra Large Big Mama pantyhose, $2.49; also in sheer stretch Lycra® Spandex support pantyhose, $3.49: suggested retail prices.

R

Captiva Panty Hose, 1972

Fancy up your legs with these smart new fashion knee highs from Beverly Jane. Choose from a dazzling array of styles and colors, cuffed and uncuffed. Then, pull up your socks. And step out in style. Hanes-Mills. P.O. Box 2105, High Point, North Carolina 27261.

Hanes — Red Label®

FANCY FOOTWORK.

Hanes Socks, 1977

Make your legs look good. And feel good, too.

With Sheer Energy® Pantyhose. Our sheer smooth yarn makes your legs look good. Our all-day massage™ makes your legs feel good.

So get into sheer, smooth Sheer Energy. (Now you can get 'em in our Queensize, too.)

SHEER ENERGY

Sheer Energy Panty Hose, 1977

Join the Dexter movement for the abolishment of drab, dreary, old fashioned, discombobulated, depressing, outdated footwear.

DEXTER

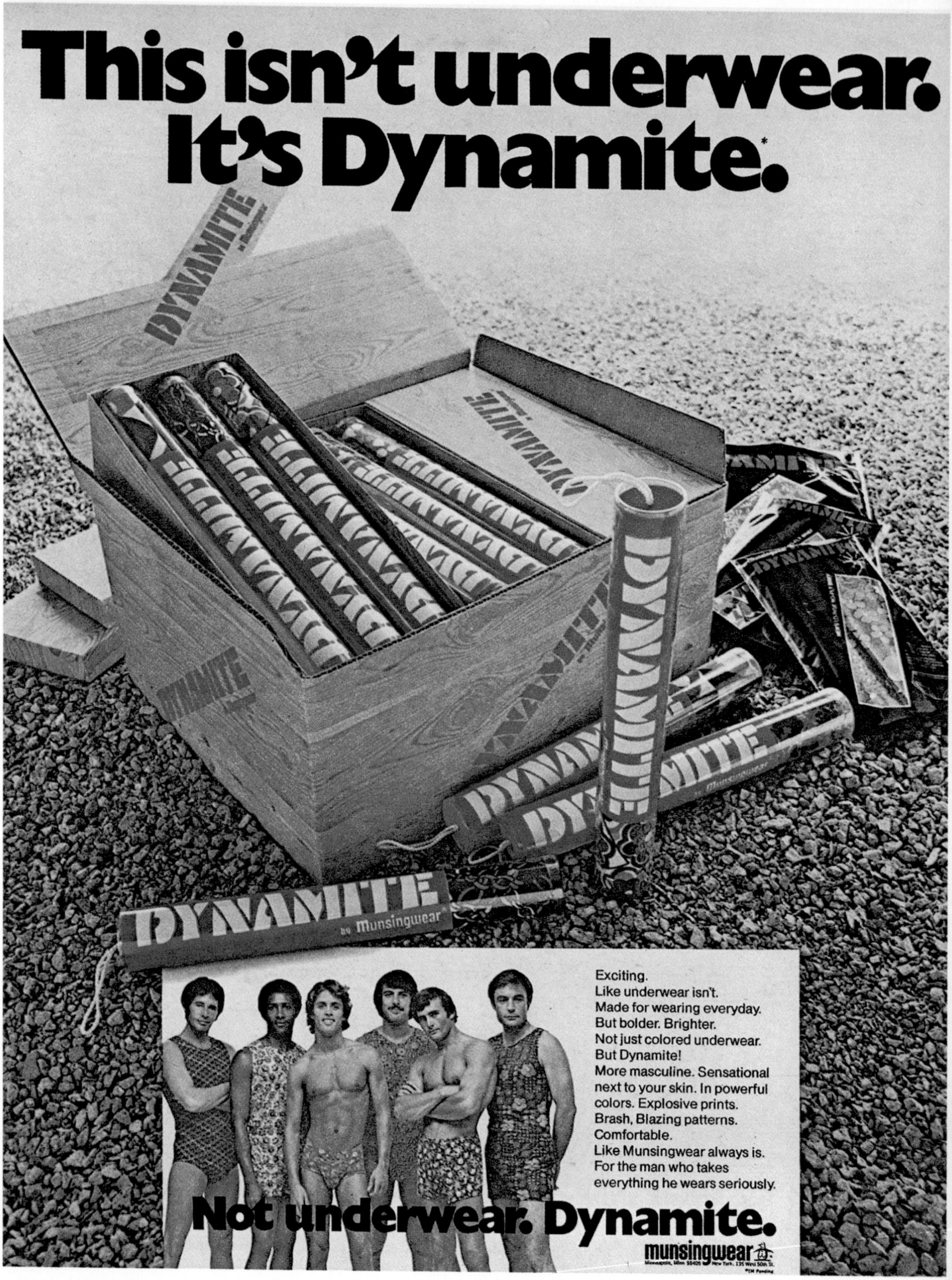

This isn't underwear. It's Dynamite.*

Exciting.
Like underwear isn't.
Made for wearing everyday.
But bolder. Brighter.
Not just colored underwear.
But Dynamite!
More masculine. Sensational
next to your skin. In powerful
colors. Explosive prints.
Brash, Blazing patterns.
Comfortable.
Like Munsingwear always is.
For the man who takes
everything he wears seriously.

Not underwear. Dynamite.

munsingwear
Minneapolis, Minn 55405 New York, 135 West 50th St.
*TM Pending

Dynamite Underwear, 1973

▶ *Dingo Boots, 1977*

Hard drivin' and fast livin' can
leave a man plumb wore out. But his
Levi's for Feet boots will
keep goin' strong.

Levi's for feet

Available in fine stores everywhere

Levi's®

STEP UP TO ADIDAS

adidas can make any youngster an "Allstar." All adidas sport-shoes, tracksuits and rainsuits are designed and developed with the aid of the best athletes in the world.
adidas – a must for fun and success in sports!

adidas®

More information available at your next sporting goods dealer or write to:

Adidas Athletic Shoes, 1975

The City Cowboy Collection

Fashion excitement! The Look for Fall. Nobody brings the West to the city better than that designer of finely-crafted leather footwear, Giorgio Brutini. What are you waiting for, pardner?

GIORGIO BRUTINI
paris   madrid   são paulo   harbor IMPORTS
A Division of

350 Fifth Avenue, N.Y.C. (212) 695-3880

the stores listed .

Giorgio Brutini Boots, 1979

I'd like to be a Star!

Look at the top stars in basketball, baseball, football and other sports. They are winning in adidas – the brand with the 3 stripes. However, adidas training shoes and suits are not only worn for sports, adidas makes the scene at home, on vacation, on the run or just taking it easy.

Why not? adidas is great for everything – casual and comfortable. adidas has a big choice in all colors and sizes, something for everybody. Call your local adidas dealer or write to:

adidas®

Levi's Boots, 1979 ◄   *Adidas Athletic Shoes, 1973*

NOCONA BOOTS

Ask for Nocona Boots where quality western boots are sold. Style shown #4781. With No. 6 toe it's Style #1242.
NOCONA BOOT COMPANY · ENID JUSTIN, PRESIDENT · DEPT. GQ4781 · BOX 599 · NOCONA, TEXAS 76255 · (817) 825-3321
† Where to buy it? See page 235

Nocona Boots, 1979

You'll get a boot out of this.
$5.88 a pair.

Where can you possibly find hook and eyelet lace-up boots, with side zippers, stretch shiny vinyl uppers, 1½ inch man-made heel, man-made soles, 16 inches high for $5.88 a pair?

At Wards. If you're ready for a boot, we're ready

for you. In brown, black and white.

Open a Wards "Charg-All" account. It makes shopping simpler in our stores and catalogs.

MONTGOMERY
WARD

Wards. The unexpected.

You Can
Judge
A Man
By
His Boots

NUNN BUSH
Brass Boot®

new orleans · new york · rochester
dallas · denver · houston · milwaukee
atlanta · berkeley · beverly hills · chicago
sausalito · san francisco · washington d.c.

Montgomery Ward Department Store, 1971 ◄

Nunn Bush Boots, 1971

Converse Coach in suede and canvas

the basketball shoe that keeps going... on and off the court.

It's a quality basketball shoe... it's a rugged, handsome all around athletic shoe. In suede, canvas and sharp new team colors, the Converse Coach performs like a pro on the court and keeps going ... off the court, on any surface hard or soft, for a game of touch, mowing the lawn, jogging, you name it. The new suede Coach is in cool, supple, napped glove leather for beautiful, long-lasting comfort, and it boasts a padded

tongue and ankle collar for snug, foot-hugging fit. Both the suede and canvas models offer full heel and arch cushion and comfortable sponge insole. Plus the special Converse sole design and compound for a sure grip and extra long wear. Suede Coach in natural, blue, gold and black Oxford. Canvas Coach in black and white Hi-Top and Oxford. More sports heroes from Converse.

See the Converse dealer nearest you — listed on the left.

★ **converse**

Converse Athletic Shoes, 1971

HOW DO YOU STEP INTO YOUR BACKHAND SO NICELY, CHRIS?

Chris Evert steps in Chris Evert™ shoes by Converse, the shoes of the stars. Chris wanted new comfort, new style, and exceptional stress support for the toughest tennis competition in the world. She got what she wanted. Stars and stripes and everything nice.

★ **CONVERSE**
THE SHOES OF THE STARS
an **Eltra** company

Converse Athletic Shoes, 1977

"I can play better than you. 'Cause I practice every day. I wear P.F. Flyers. And my dad is Hank Aaron."

When your dad is Hank Aaron, you get a lot of good tips on how to play a better game. Like wearing a shoe that helps you outplay the competition.

That's why Hank Aaron, right fielder for the Atlanta Braves, has young Hank wear P.F. Flyers. Because they help young Hank to run faster, cut sharper and keep going longer.

It's the Posture Foundation® wedge inside each heel that does it, by helping feet to work the right way. The Posture Foundation is what the P.F in our name stands for. And only our shoes have it.

So take a hint from young Hank Aaron.

Get your dad to buy you P.F. Flyers.

P.F

P.F. FLYERS.
The only one with the wedge.

BFGoodrich *...a forward of excellence*

P. F. Flyers Athletic Shoes, 1971

Our proving grounds.

Proving that the Forest Hills is adidas' lightest and most advanced tennis shoe required a unique series of scientific experiments: championship tennis matches. Matches which helped verify that its 8.7 ounce* weight made it easier to keep going...even after three gruelling hours.

Matches that aided in demonstrating the sophisticated adjustable sole ventilation system could keep inside temperatures 20% lower.

Matches that assisted in proving the specially developed Polaire sole to be five times more durable than ordinary soles.

The adidas Forest Hills. It took everything science knew about tennis and turned it to your advantage.

*Men's size 8½.

The Forest Hills adidas' lightest tennis shoe

adidas ✦
The science of sport.

Adidas Athletic Shoes, 1979

Guess what inspired these new shoes.

The Indy 500.
It's a speed package crafted after the great high performance cars. A new shoe design inspired by the wild and mean machines.
Get into one where you buy fine footwear. Rev it up.

The Purcell RaceAround.
All the things that belong to the track now belong to this new shoe.
It's custom designed for movin' out. And movin' in.
All leather exterior. Air cooled. Cushion soles. Bumper-like toe guard. Tough rubber tread. Body by B. F. Goodrich.
On the rack. At your Purcell dealer's. Along with more than twenty other Purcell styles and colors to choose from.

Get it on.

Jack Purcell

Jack Purcell Shoes, 1972

The best double coverage on the court. Wigwam Socks and Converse All Stars.®

Wigwam Socks and Converse All Stars. They work together for fit, feel, support, and comfort. From one end of the court to the other.

Wigwam Socks come high or low, in different styles and colors to match your All Stars.

Converse All Stars, high-cut or low, in smooth leather, suede or canvas, in your team colors. To match your Wigwams.

Put your best feet forward this season. Put them in Wigwam Socks and Converse All Stars.

Wigwam Socks and Converse All Stars.

Converse Athletic Shoes/Wigwam Socks, 1974

The Olympic Pacesetters

Look at the feet and your eyes will convince you that more olympic athletes wear adidas than all other brands combined. The secret is that adidas makes the right shoe for the right event.

adidas®
—the original 3-stripe shoe.

Adidas Athletic Shoes, 1976

Five women who can easily afford any fur coat in the world tell why they're proudly wearing fakes.

DORIS DAY: *"Killing an animal to make a coat is a sin. It wasn't meant to be, and we have no right to do it.*
"At one time, before I was aware of the situation, I did buy fur coats. Today when I look at them hanging in the closet I could cry.
"It's so wrong for a man to think that the biggest thing he can do for his wife is buy her a fur coat at Christmas. It's the most evil thing he can do. Buy her a fake fur. They're so beautiful, so lovely, so warm, so pretty to look at.
"A woman gains status when she refuses to see anything killed to be put on her back. Then she's truly beautiful..."

AMANDA BLAKE: *"The wearing of any kind of skins—even the kind that are supposedly raised for fur, like mink or sable—is something I just don't believe in. Killing animals for vanity I think is a shame.*
"I feel very guilty about having worn fur coats. As for the women who know about our vanishing wildlife and continue to buy fur coats—I wonder how they'd like to be skinned?
"I have noticed that the reaction to real fur coats is becoming nausea on the observer's part. If a woman wants to wear something that looks like an animal, fake fur is the only way to go.
"People are putting the whole real fur thing down and I thank God...thank God."

JAYNE MEADOWS: *"I don't see how you can wear a fur coat without feeling, literally, like a murderer. It is, I believe, against God's law. Against His whole plan for the universe.*
"I feel very sad for women who continue to purchase real fur coats. They are lacking in a woman's most important requisites, heart and sensitivity.
"Bravo for the women who are wearing fake fur. It's the only way to go. It's warmer and everything else. And you are happy with it because you don't feel guilty in it. You don't feel like a murderer."

ANGIE DICKINSON: *"Although I don't feel I have the right to tell other people what to do, my respect for an animal's right to live doesn't let me approve of the killing of animals for coats.*
"If a woman can help an animal or a child, that's the most important thing."

MARY TYLER MOORE: *"The killing of an animal for the sake of the appearance of luxury doesn't achieve anything. I have seen so many coats so much more attractive than fur—some fake fur, some fabric. It's in the design, not necessarily the fabric.*
"I am aware that there are specific ecological problems, but for me all animals have a right to humane treatment.

"Someday, soon I hope, the killing of an animal for fur will hold for us the same revulsion we feel, say, when we hear those horrible stories about parts of the world where they open the top of a live monkey's skull and pour hot lead in because it's supposed to improve the flavor of the meat."

E. F. Timme & Son is one of the world's leading suppliers of plush and flat fabrics for home, industry and transportation.
A single Timme-Tation fake fur represents only a small part of our output and income, it is the subject of virtually all our advertising.
For two reasons:
1. We believe that the slaughter of wildlife in the name of fashion is cruel and, eventually, suicidal. We want to do something about it. As we gain acceptance for fake fur through advertising, the demand for the real thing goes down. So fewer animals die.
And that's the big thing.
2. As more and more people start turning to fake fur, we want them to know that E. F. Timme & Son makes the best fake fur money can buy. 45 different kinds. With heavy emphasis, we don't mind adding, on the Endangered Species.
Incidentally, we only make the fabric. It's the many fine manufacturers and designers who buy from us who make the coats. Miss Day's "Lynx," Miss Blake's "Hair Seal," Miss Meadows' "Leopard," Miss Dickinson's "Jaguar," Miss Moore's "Tiger" were designed and executed by Lupa in Timme-Tation Lynx, Silver Frost, Congo, Jagra and Bengal.

TIMME-TATION FAKE FUR.
E. F. TIMME & SON, INC.
200 MADISON AVENUE, NEW YORK CITY
CLEAN BY FUR COAT METHOD ONLY

Fur coats shouldn't be made of fur.

These ladies have received no payment for their appearance in this ad. At their request a contribution has been made by the E. F. Timme Co. to Cleveland Amory's Fund For Animals. These ladies are all on the national board of that organization. For information on how you can join, write Fund For Animals, Inc., Box 444, Wall Street Station, N.Y.C.

Timme-Tation Fake Fur, 1971

It doesn't cost a million to feel like a million.

How you feel depends on some self-appraisal. Which one is you?
1. The Norwegian Blue Fox jacket with leather trim. $325.
2. The Red Fox paw with the Gray Fox collar. $950.
3. The dark Ranch Mink cape. $4500.
4. The pale beige Mink poncho. $3500.
5. The natural Stone Marten coat. $4000.
6. The natural Muskrat with Canadian Lynx. $695.
7. The multi-colored Chinese Rabbit. $125.
8. The pale Mink safari jacket. $3500.
9. The green-dyed Fox. $2500.
10. The bleached white Mink. $5000.
11. The chestnut Mink coat. $2900.
12. The Natural Russian Sable. $25,000.
13. The multi-colored Mink tail poncho, trimmed with Raccoon. $950.
14. The chubby of natural Red Fox ovals. $250.
15. The beige Mink paw with Canadian Lynx. $1100.
16. The chestnut Mink coat. $3500.
17. The hooded Lynx Cat topper. $1095.
18. The Russian White Fitch Coat. $3250.
19. The dark Ranch Mink. $5000.
20. The brown Persian Lamb with Blue Fox. $950.
What does it take to make you feel like a million? All it takes is Fur. Real Fur.

Fur.

American Fur Industry, 1972

▶ Blackglama Furs, 1973

What becomes a Legend most?

Blackglama

HOW THE WEST WAS WON

Out of the West comes a look that is changing the way America
dresses. It's bright, bold, sassy and sweet. And, the Gap's
got it. Straight leg denims, bright knits, earth tone vests in
burlap or suede, and the new look in overalls. Discover the
fashion look of the West at The Gap. You'll be glad you did

We asked our photographer to put <u>all</u> our denim in one picture. He couldnt. *Levi's*

Pandora Women's Wear, 1970

Coats & Clark Wool, 1972

Springmaid Fabric, 1970

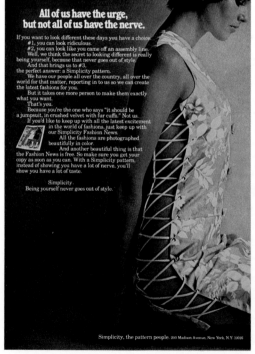

Simplicity Patterns, 1970

Levi's, 1971

Dressing.
As easy as one, two, three.

Three pieces.
All sweater ribbed.
Cardigan jacket. White collared
top. And pants.

All 100% polyester doubleknit.
Machine wash-and-dryable.

Exclusively ours.
Under $36.
In misses sizes 8 to 18.

At most Sears, Roebuck and Co.
larger stores.

You'll find lots more
where this came from
in our Dress Department.
Come try on.

Sears
GREAT LOOKING
Dresses

Sears Department Store, 1973

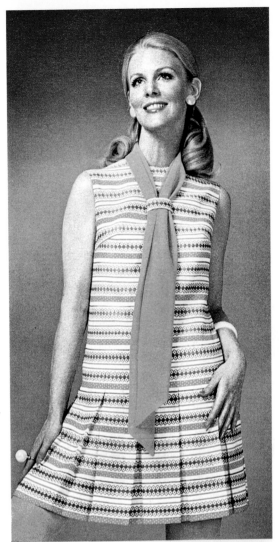

R & K

ORIGINALS

for the girl who knows . . .

A breeze of sheer voile, striped and scarfed and swished with pleats.
65% **DACRON*** polyester-35% cotton. Green/purple (shown), gold/
black, red/blue. Sizes 10 to 18. About $30. **R & K Originals**, 1400
Broadway, New York, N. Y. 10018, a Division of Jonathan Logan.

*DU PONT REGISTERED TRADEMARK.   SLIGHTLY HIGHER IN THE WEST.

R & K Originals Dresses, 1970

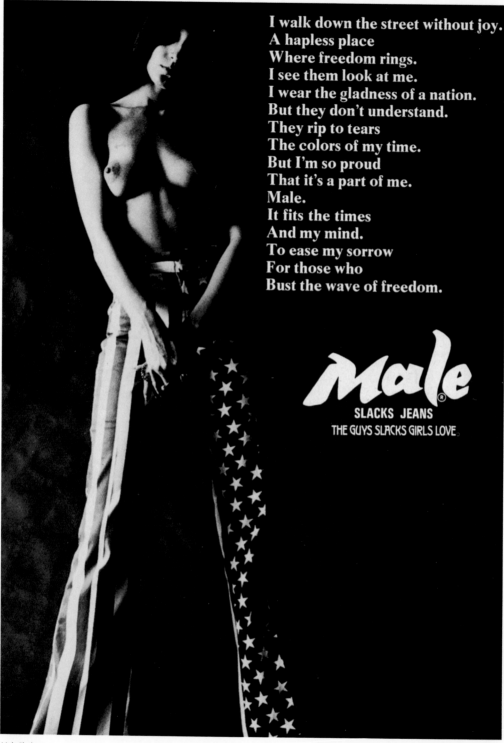

I walk down the street without joy.
A hapless place
Where freedom rings.
I see them look at me.
I wear the gladness of a nation.
But they don't understand.
They rip to tears
The colors of my time.
But I'm so proud
That it's a part of me.
Male.
It fits the times
And my mind.
To ease my sorrow
For those who
Bust the wave of freedom.

Male
SLACKS JEANS
THE GUYS SLACKS GIRLS LOVE

Male Slacks, 1971

London Britches Stores, 1970

ENTERTAINERS.

Look for Turtle Bax. You'll find easy-living clothes that say spring is in the air. Cool crop tops for all the freedom under the sun. . .denim with playful lace. . .and super skirts just for the fun of it all. Yes Turtle Bax are still priced like ordinary clothes.

Left, Petticoat Junction. Jeans about $13, top about $8.50. Right. Mood Indigo. Skirt about $12, top about $8.

You'll find these and all the other exciting Turtle Bax looks for spring at stores everywhere that sell fun fashions.

Turtle Bax
Priced like ordinary clothes.

turtle bax

A product of Washington Manufacturing Co.
Nashville, Tennessee

Funky Fashions, 1978 ◄

Turtle Bax Clothing, 1975

257

Are you the right kind of woman for it?

Can you brew bathtub gin?

Can you light his fire swiveling to a calypso beat while slugging champagne from a bottle and wearing nothing but one Edwardian rose behind your ear?

Find something to talk about when the TV set goes on the blink?

Do you *have* to have your carrot juiced every morning?

Own at least one pair of strategically cut-out bikini panties?

Have you a perceptive eye, a mind like a calculator, a bent for men who dig bikini panties, a passion for Fibber McGee, a cool head for business and an obsession for snakeskin backgammon boards?

Will you say "Yes" to a summer at sea even though you get seasick taking a bath?

Promise to love, honor and seduce him with caviar, rum swizzles and suckling pig on your anniversary that *he* forgot?

Be first on the block with an ocelot?

Do a striptease without giggling?

See a psychiatrist if he does?

Did you say you knew the male silkworm moth (*Bombyx mori*) can detect the female's scent from 6.8 miles upwind?

You did?

Congratulations.

You get the idea.

Why not get in touch with the Mistress Collection: call toll-free 800-421-2062.*

Tell the operator you're ready for Funky's new Alfresco Group in sensual nylon jersey. She'll tell you where to go.

In California call: 213-749-1481.

*Except Alaska & Hawaii

The Mistress Collection by Funky.

Funky. Executive Offices: 1053 South Main Street, Los Angeles, California 90015

Funky Fashions, 1974

▶ *Christian Dior Swimwear, 1977*

WANGENHEIM

Electrifying is Your Dior.

Frederick's of Hollywood, 1975

Frederick's of Hollywood, 1978

Frederick's of Hollywood, 1974

Be a panty nut.
For peanuts.

Clip them out and see how great they look. Then—for about a dollar a pair—buy yourself a wardrobe-ful. All of luxurious, absorbent, *healthier* Eiderlon (50% Dacron® trilobal polyester, 50% combed cotton). We guarantee you'll love them. Or return them to us with your sales receipt within 30 days for a *full refund*.

eiderlon®
IN 1001 TEMPTING STYLES

Eiderlon Panties, 1978

"Peace in '70" for $2.75

Show how you feel.
Get your "Peace in '70" Sweatshirts.
A top quality, shrink-proof Sweatshirt.
In dove white and love red.
Long and short sleeves available in S,M,L,XL.
From the man who bottles Coca-Cola to you for only $2.75.
Wear it in peace. And while you're at it,
have an ice-cold Coca-Cola. It's the real thing.

Peace in 1970

Send $2.75 for each Sweatshirt together with one proof-purchase seal from any carton of Coke in cans or no-depo
no-return bottles.
  Send to SWEATSHIRT:
      Box 779
      Darien, Connecticut 06820
Please send me ☐ Sweatshirt(s): Long sleeve ☐   Short sleeve ☐
Small ☐ Medium ☐ Large ☐ X Large ☐
Name
Street
City _____ State _____ Zip _

Cool-Ray Sunglasses, 1970

Riviera Eyewear, 1974

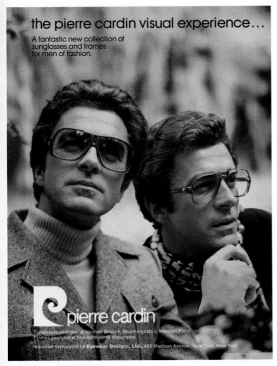

Peace In '70 Sweatshirt, 1970 ◄

Pierre Cardin Eyewear, 1976

Polo Lifestyle Eyewear, 1977

A direct hit from the **Christian Dior** sunglass coll

CHRIS VON

Explosive is Your Dior.

INTRODUCING THE
World's first cologne
exclusively for gay men.

REO

WORLD'S FIRST COLOGNE
EXCLUSIVELY FOR GAY MEN

...our Christmas gift to you. With every purchase we'll include the custom designed Reo Pendant with your order. (Expires Dec. 31)

24 Kt., Plate

REO PRODUCTS, INC. P.O. Box 2766, Orlando, Fla. 32802

Enclosed please find $ _____ (check or money order), for _____ bottles at $12 each. Florida residents please add 4% sales tax. Foreign orders, add $1.50.

Ship to

Name _____

Address _____

City _____

State/Zip _____

Gift Purchases   A

We'll ship to above address with card stating "Greetings from..." Print your name, clearly, below

_____

Christian Dior Sunglasses, 1977 ◀   *REO Cologne, 1978*

Food & Beverage
266

General Foods International Coffees Introduces:

New Irish Mocha Mint.
"Lucky us."

"If you love the flavors of chocolate and mint as much as I do, you're in luck. New Irish Mocha Mint is coffee with a rich, chocolatey flavor and an elegant touch of mint. Delicious. Soothing. Of course, I love the other flavors, too. Orange Cappuccino with an enticing aroma of orange, chocolatey flavored Suisse Mocha, cinnamony Cafe Vienna, and smooth Café Francais.

But for chocolate and mint lovers, new Irish Mocha Mint is a special treat. Lucky us!"

—Carol Lawrence

International Coffee, 1978

Perk up!

We've made a Max-Pax® just for you.

Max-Pax has *two* blends of coffee for you to choose from—one for regular percolators and one for electric percolators.

And Max-Pax is the only coffee that comes in a filter to trap grounds and sediment, things that can turn coffee bitter.

So no matter which blend you perk up, you get a great first cup...and it even tastes good after *six hours* in the pot.

Get yourself some Max-Pax, Range-Top® blend or Electra-Perk® blend.

If Max-Pax tastes good even after six hours, imagine how delicious it tastes just perked.

Max-Pax Coffee, 1975

Have you tried Mountain Grown Folger's?

Folger's Coffee and Folger's Flaked Coffee—two great coffees, one delicious taste.

Folger's Coffee comes in 3 grinds—regular, electric perc and drip.

Folger's Flaked Coffee is specially designed for automatic drip coffeemakers.

Folger's tastes so delicious, it's the leading coffee in most of the country. Has been for years. Folger's is specially blended to give you a rich, full flavor no other coffee quite matches. Its aroma is so rich, you can even smell how delicious it tastes. And Folger's is mountain grown. There's nothing better for coffee than fresh mountain air and sunshine. In fact, mountain grown is the richest, most aromatic kind of coffee there is.

Folger's Flaked Coffee is specially designed for automatic drip coffeemakers. It's the same delicious Mountain Grown Folger's. But it's flaked to release more rich flavor—so you use less. If you normally use 5 measures per pot, you only need 4 measures of Folger's Flaked Coffee. So the 13 ounce can makes as many cups as a full pound. Try delicious Folger's Coffee or Folger's Flaked Coffee. They're both 100% pure coffee.

Taste how rich and delicious coffee can be. Mountain Grown Folger's.

Burger King, 1972 ◄

Folger's Coffee, 1978

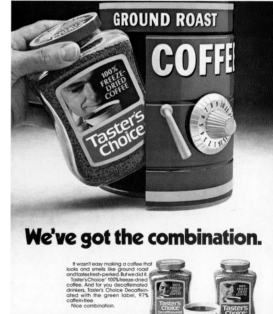

GROUND ROAST COFFEE

We've got the combination.

It wasn't easy making a coffee that looks and smells like ground roast and tastes fresh-perked. But we did it. Taster's Choice® 100% freeze-dried coffee. And for you decaffeinated drinkers, Taster's Choice Decaffeinated with the green label, 97% caffeine-free.

Nice combination.

We look, smell and taste like ground roast.

Taster's Choice Coffee, 1974

The quiet strength
of the earth . . .

brought to your teacup by our unique herb tea blends.

available in health and natural food stores, and most grocery stores
in the bay area.

Celestial Seasonings Herbal Tea, 1975

► *Sanka Instant Coffee, 1972*

What makes Hi-C the sensible drink?
The fresh fruit it's made from?
The fact that it's naturally sweetened?
Or is it all that vitamin C?
It's all this. And more. Hi-C is loved by the <u>whole</u> family.
No wonder Hi-C is the sensible drink...
it makes sense for everyone.

The Sensible drink

Hi-C Grape Drink, 1970

Wow! I could've had a V-8

Taking a break? V-8 Cocktail Vegetable Juice is a healthful blend of 8 vegetables that tastes terrific and is naturally low in calories. Only 35 calories a 6-ounce serving.

Remember, the time to think of having "V-8" is before you've had something else.

V-8 Vegetable Juice, 1978

Coke *adds life...*
to Randy and Sue... and their sandwiches, too!

Coca-Cola, 1977

Coca-Cola, 1978   ▶ *Perrier Sparkling Water, 1977*

Naturally sparkling from the center of the earth.

Today, Man artificially carbonates his drinks and mixers.
But *not* Perrier.
The miracle of Perrier is *natural carbonation:*
Lighter, more refreshing and more delicate than any made by Man.
That "miracle" takes place deep below the surface of the earth in Southern France near Vergeze. There, delicate gasses—trapped over 140 million years ago in the volcanic eruptions of the Cretaceous Era—are released and rise through porous limestone and cracked marls to add natural life and sparkle to the icy waters of a single spring: *Source Perrier.*

The result is Perrier.
Bottled directly from Nature. With no chemicals, preservatives, flavorings or additives of any type.
And no calories.
100% natural Perrier.
Pure refreshment served chilled with a slice of fresh lemon or a wedge of lime. So versatile it adds "the sparkle of champagne" to fine wines. And, with imported spirits, is the mixer *par excellence.*
Imported Perrier.
It is the product of Nature and the love of France.
Enjoy it in good health.

"Everything is in this new buttermilk
pancake mix—even egg and shortening.
All you add is water to bake up golden fluffy
pancakes or crisp hearty waffles." *Betty Crocker*

The Product 19 Story.

As America has become more nutrition-conscious, more people than ever are discovering Product 19.®

It is one of the country's leading high nutrition cereals.

Much of the story is on the front of the box.

The rest of the story is in the taste.

Product 19 is a delicious blend of four grains—corn, rice, wheat and oats.

The firm texture and pleasing taste have won thousands of new friends of all ages.

Kellogg invites you to join the growing number of people who are discovering how good tasting a high nutrition cereal can be.

You get **100%** of the officially established minimum daily adult requirements for **VITAMINS** and **IRON** in one serving (1 oz.) of Product 19.

Kellogg's
PRODUCT
19

A tasty blend of corn, rice, wheat, and oats with defatted wheat germ added

You get **100%** of the officially established minimum daily adult requirements for **VITAMINS** and **IRON** in one serving (1 oz.) of Product 19. (See Side Panel)

® Kellogg Company © 1971 by Kellogg Company

Betty Crocker Pancake Mix, 1970 ◄   Kellogg's Product 19 Cereal, 1971   ► Carnation Instant Breakfast, 1970   ►► Hungry Jack Biscuits, 1975

275

Foster Farms Chicken, 1970

Campbell's Pork & Beans, 1970

Chef Boy-ar-dee Pizza Mix, 1973

Stove Top Stuffing Mix, 1978

HAWAII
As close as the Campbell's Soup on your shelf.

Island-Style Chicken

1 can (about 8 ounces) pineapple chunks in heavy syrup	2 teaspoons soy sauce
2 pounds chicken parts	1 large clove garlic, minced
2 tablespoons shortening	1 medium green pepper, cut in squares
1 can Campbell's Chicken Broth	3 tablespoons cornstarch
¼ cup vinegar	¼ cup water
2 tablespoons brown sugar	

Drain pineapple chunks, reserving syrup. In skillet, brown chicken in shortening; pour off fat. Add reserved syrup, broth, vinegar, sugar, soy and garlic. Cover; cook over low heat 40 minutes. Add green pepper and pineapple chunks; cook 5 minutes more or until done. Stir occasionally. Combine cornstarch and water; gradually stir into sauce. Cook, stirring until thickened. Serve with cooked parsleyed rice. Makes 4 servings.

Cookbook offer: There's a world of good cooking waiting for you in Campbell's "Cooking with Soup" cookbook. Over 600 recipes fill this beautiful 200-page, hard-covered book. Just send $1.50 and two Campbell's Soup labels with your name, address, and zip code to: COOKBOOK, Box 9861C, Maple Plain, Minn. 55348. Offer good only in U.S.A. Allow 6 weeks for delivery.

A world of good cooking brought home with Campbell's.

Campbell's Soup, 1978

MEXiCO
As close as the Campbell's Soup on your shelf.

Campbell Soup Company, Camden, N.J. 08101 U.S.A.

Mexicanos Tacos

2 lb. ground beef	24 tacos shells
½ cup chopped green pepper	Shredded Cheddar or Monterey Jack cheese
1 can Campbell's Chili Beef Soup	Shredded lettuce
1 can Campbell's Tomato Soup	Chopped onion Diced tomato
1 to 2 tbsp. finely chopped cherry peppers	

In skillet, brown beef and cook green pepper until tender; stir to separate meat. Add soups and cherry peppers. Cook over low heat 5 minutes; stir occasionally. Fill each taco shell with 3 to 4 tablespoons meat mixture; top each with remaining ingredients. Makes 24 tacos.

Cookbook offer: For a hard-covered copy of Campbell's "Cooking with Soup" cookbook with over 600 recipes in it, send $1.50 and 2 Campbell's Soup labels with your name, address and zip code to: COOKBOOK, Box 1981J, Maple Plain, Minn. 55348. Wisconsin residents send $1.50 and label facsimiles only. Offer good only in U.S.A. Allow 6 weeks for delivery.

A world of good cooking brought home with Campbell's.

Campbell's Soup, 1978

La Choy makes Chop Suey Vegetables "Swing American" in

Linda's Tuna Bake

2 tablespoons butter	1½ cups (one 16 oz. can) La Choy Chop Suey Vegetables, rinsed, drained
¼ cup chopped green pepper	
1 tablespoon flour	
1 teaspoon salt	1 can (6½ to 7 ounces) tuna, drained, flaked
½ teaspoon pepper	
½ cup milk	2 medium tomatoes, cut in wedges
1 egg, slightly beaten	
¼ cup dairy sour cream	2 tablespoons butter
½ cup mayonnaise	
½ cup crushed La Choy Chow Mein Noodles	

Melt 2 tablespoons butter in saucepan; add green pepper and cook 2 minutes. Blend in flour, salt and pepper. Gradually add milk; cook, stirring until slightly thickened. Blend together egg, sour cream and mayonnaise; stir into sauce. Add vegetables and tuna. Turn into buttered 1-quart baking dish. Arrange tomato wedges on top. Bake at 375° for 25 minutes. Melt 2 tablespoons butter in skillet; add Chow Mein Noodles and heat until lightly browned. Sprinkle over top of Tuna Bake.

4 TO 5 SERVINGS.

Another "Swing American" Idea:

La Choy Frozen Egg Rolls are great as appetizers or snacks anytime.

© La Choy Food Products

La Choy Chop Suey Vegetables, 1978   ▸ *Chicken of the Sea Tuna, 1971*

Do you believe in mermaids?
A lot of people do.

Just ask any mermaid
you happen to see
What's the best tuna?
"It's Chicken of the Sea."

Look for Chicken of the Sea Frozen Shrimp, too!

Porkfest with pork chops

...it's a Natural!

FRUIT GLAZED BUTTERFLY CHOPS

6	pork butterfly chops,	2	tablespoons golden raisins
	cut 1 inch thick	⅓	cup cream sherry
1	package (11 ounces)	½	teaspoon dry mustard
	mixed dried fruit	½	teaspoon ground ginger
1½	cups white catawba	1	tablespoon cornstarch
	grape juice	2	tablespoons cold water

In medium saucepan, combine dried fruit, grape juice, raisins, sherry, mustard, and ginger. Bring to boiling. Cover; reduce heat and simmer till fruit is plump and tender, about 25 to 30 minutes. Meanwhile, place butterfly chops on rack in broiler pan. Broil at moderate temperature 3 to 4 inches from heat till done, about 25 minutes, turning once. In small bowl, combine cornstarch and cold water. Stir into fruit mixture. Cook, stirring constantly, over moderate heat till mixture is thickened and bubbly. Cook 1 minute longer. Serve fruit sauce with chops. Makes 6 servings.

When it comes to giving you a choice, pork's just the thing. Chops alone come in a variety of cuts including rib, loin, butterfly, boneless, as well as smoked, just to mention a few. Mmmm . . . delicious. And pork offers plenty of protein, iron, and B vitamins, too.

FREE For a free 32-page recipe book "Pork for Two" (it has recipes for more than two, too), send a self-addressed, stamped, business envelope to: National Pork Producers Council, P.O. Box 10351, Des Moines, Iowa 50306. You'll discover pork's a natural for breakfast, brunch and lunch time, dinner time, snack time, any time. Offer good in U.S.A. only.

National Pork Producers Council, 1978

Make a Magnificent Melt-Over with Cheese

What's easier to make yet harder to top than cheese melt-overs? Just turn your imagination loose and get cookin'. You could become the most creative cook on the block. Because cheese goes with just about everything. From hot dogs to casseroles to fancy hors d'oeuvres. Just slice it thin and let your creativity begin. You'll find there are hundreds of food and cheese combinations you'll melt over.

Cheddar Hot Dog Melt-Over

Your own cheese dog made to order. And as easy to make as it is to love. Just cut a slice of Cheddar cheese into three strips. Place over a frankfurter in a bun. Broil until cheese spreads over the frankfurter and presto! Kids love 'em. Everyone does. The tangy Cheddar makes the dog with just the right bite.

american dairy association®

Ortega Products, 1971 ◄   *American Dairy Association, 1978*

HOW TO WIN COMPLIMENTS, COMPLIMENTS OF SPAM.

It's easy to win compliments when you start with SPAM® Luncheon Meat. Because SPAM can be the start of a whole world of good things. Put it in a casserole. Add it to a salad. Make it into a midnight snack. Dice it up with eggs. Or fry it up by itself.

Our special blend of pork shoulder and Hormel ham can really make a meal. And it's the perfect ingredient for your food budget.

PINEAPPLE SPAM LOAF

1 can (12-oz.) SPAM® Luncheon Meat
1 can (8-oz.) pineapple slices
¼ cup brown sugar
¼ tsp. dry mustard

Cut four slices almost, but not quite, all the way through SPAM loaf. Cut pineapple slices in half and place one halved slice in each of the slits in the SPAM. Place loaf in small pie pan or shallow casserole; arrange remaining pineapple around SPAM. Combine brown sugar and dry mustard mixture with two tbsp. pineapple juice; spoon over SPAM. Bake in pre-heated 350° oven for 25-30 minutes, basting occasionally. Makes four servings.

Eat the basic 4 foods every day.

A LOT OF MEALS. BUT NOT A LOT OF MONEY.

Spam Canned Meat, 1978

GERMAN PIZZA

No one has to tell you how great pizza tastes. Especially when you make it with Chef Boy-ar-dee, the world's most popular pizza mix.

Just thinking about the freshly baked dough, the rich pizza sauce and tangy cheese is enough to make anyone hungry.

And you can vary Chef Boy-ar-dee Cheese Pizza Mix in so many ways.

Just make it according to directions and in the last five minutes of baking, vary the toppings.

You can make German Pizza by adding sliced knockwurst and sauerkraut (rinsed and drained). Then sprinkle generously with caraway seeds.

Polynesian Pizza: Top with chopped cooked ham and green pepper (browned together in a skillet) and small pineapple chunks.

Indian Pizza: Begin by adding ¼ to ½ teaspoon of curry powder (according to taste) to the pizza sauce, then top in the last five minutes of baking with chopped cooked (or canned) chicken and chopped green pepper. Sprinkle on nuts and raisins.

 Chef Boy-ar-dee. The world's most popular pizza mix.

Chef Boy-ar-dee Pizza Mix, 1973

▶ *McDonald's, 1973* ▶ ▶ *McDonald's, 1979*

283

Get Down with Something Good at McDonald's.

Carver Day Camp Gettin' Down.
    Field trips are always a lot of fun.
Especially if you stop by McDonald's on your way home.
Because when it comes to good eatin',
McDonald's is one place that will satisfy everybody.
On the real side, kids can really dig
gettin' down at McDonald's.

McDonald's

Have it your way

BURGER KING®

Surprise your big eaters with something serious. Bring home a Whopper from Burger King.® Regular or Double Beef Whopper. Either way, it's got lots of juicy, real broiled beef. Have it with all the trimmings or fixed just the way you like it. For a change of taste, let us whip some cheese on it. Have mercy!! When the appetite's big, get a Whopper at Burger King. Regular or Double Beef. And Have It Your Way.® It's the only way.

...make it a Whopper.®

Almond Blossom Ham
Simple and simply delicious with Hormel Cure|81® Ham and Blue Diamond® Almonds.

APRICOT ALMOND GLAZE

1 can (8 oz.) pineapple tidbits in unsweetened juice	12 cloves
1 can (17 oz.) apricot halves in heavy syrup	10 allspice
	2 cinnamon sticks
1 tsp. lemon juice	½ cup Blue Diamond® Blanched Slivered
1 Tbsp. cornstarch	Almonds, toasted

While your dependable Cure/81® ham bakes, drain pineapple and reserve juice. Combine juice with apricots and syrup in blender and whirl until pureed. In medium saucepan, thoroughly blend puree, lemon juice and cornstarch. Drop spices in saucepan. Bring to a boil over medium heat, stirring constantly until thickened. Remove from heat, strain out spices. Brush hot onto ham during last half of baking. Cut pineapple tidbits in half and arrange with almonds as shown. Reheat remaining glaze, add almonds and serve as a sauce.

❖ Hormel ❖

SPRINKLE JELL-O® INSTEAD O

BRAND GELATIN

Instead of fruit sauce on ice cream or you-know-what on strawberries or "jimmies" on cup cakes. Sprinkle Jell-O Brand Gelatin right out of the box. It tastes fruity and sweet at the same time.

Sprinkle Jell-O in 15 fruity flavors. Sprinkle Orange Jell-O on strawberries or Strawberry Jell-O on ice cream or Lime Jell-O on cup cakes. Then keep what's left in your covered sugar bowl or baby food jar.

Tomorrow. Be different and ha Sprinkle Jell-O Gelatin out of t box on the things you already And you may find you can eve them better. Sprinkle. Sprinkle. Sprinkle.

It takes two to top the Waldorf.

Nothing tops it better than these two from Kraft ... Miracle Whip Salad Dressing and Kraft Miniature Marshmallows. A great combination! The lively fresh flavor of Miracle Whip and smooth blending Miniature Marshmallows add a special taste and texture to make any molded

Waldorf Crown Salad

2 3oz. pkgs. strawberry flavored gelatin
2 c. boiling water
1½ c. cold water
1 c. cubed apples
½ c. thinly sliced celery
¼ c. chopped walnuts

Dissolve gelatin in boiling water; stir in cold water. Chill until thickened; fold in remaining ingredients. Pour into 5-cup ring mold. Chill until firm. Unmold, surround with lettuce. Fill

Regal Dressing

1½ c. Kraft Miniature Marshmallows
1 c. dairy sour cream
½ c. Miracle Whip Salad Dressing

Combine ingredients: mix well. 6 to 8 servings.

Have a ball with Lindsay Olives.

And get 150 other appetizing recipes.

What could be better to get a holiday party rolling than this festive cheese ball with zesty Lindsay Ripe Olives inside and out? Here's what you'll need:

1 package cream cheese (8 oz.)
1½ cups grated mild cheddar cheese
1 jar smoke-flavored process cheese spread (5 oz.)
1 tsp. Worcestershire sauce
½ tsp. dry mustard
½ tsp. salt
1 can Lindsay Chopped Ripe Olives (7½ oz.)
Chopped parsley
1 can Lindsay Large Pitted Ripe Olives (6 oz.)

Soften cream cheese. Blend with mild cheddar cheese, cheese spread, Worcestershire sauce, mustard and salt. Beat until smooth. Fold in chopped olives and shape into ball. Decorate with Lindsay Pitted Ripe Olives, cut in halves to form petals and sprinkle with chopped parsley. Chill. Makes 1½ lb. For other exciting recipes see cookbook offer below.

Send 25¢ and one label from Lindsay Olives and we'll send you our 96-page cookbook "Lindsay Goes International."

Send to: Lindsay International, Dept. 500 (FC)
P.O. Box 278, Lindsay, California 93247

Please send me _____ cookbooks. I'm enclosing one Lindsay Olive label and 25¢ to include postage and handling for each book.

Offer expires December 31, 1974.

Lindsay. A nice town. A great olive.

Lindsay Olives, 1973

Squeez·A·Picnic

Sharp. Pimento. Hickory Smoke. Bacon. Jalapeño Pepper. Garlic. Swiss-American. In between the baseball game and the barbecue, squeeze in some good picnic snacking with Squeez-A-Snak process cheese spread from Kraft. It never needs refrigeration, so you can take it along for on-the-spot snacks in 7 flavors. Crackers, anyone?

Squeez, squeez, everybody Squeez-A-Snak.

Squeez-A-Snak Cheese Spread, 1974

When you thirst for the best.

There comes a time when alternatives just won't do. That's the time for the good, true flavor of Cracker Barrel natural cheddar cheese. Quenching your thirst never tasted better. It's another reason America spells cheese KRAFT.

Our pride. Your joy. KRAFT
Bringing good food and families together for 75 years.

Kraft Miracle Whip/Marshmallows, 1973 ◄   Cracker Barrel Cheese, 1978

CRUNCH

PREMIUM Saltines. So crisp, you won't believe your ears. Baked crisp, and kept crisp to make the good taste come through. Black Pack. So the great taste of crispness always comes through. PREMIUM Saltines, baked with enriched flour, another example of Nabisco quality.

PREMIUM **crunch** PREMIUM

The crackers with the crunch.

Premium Crackers, 1970   ► Bell Potato Chips, 1972

Please don't squeeze a bag of BELL.

They're so thin, crisp and delicious...
it's a shame to squeeze them.

Pro football teams are stuck on Chiquita® Bananas.

Collect all 26 NFL emblems.

Every single team in the National Football League now serves Chiquita Bananas as an official Training Table food.

We felt the least we can do is return the honor. So we put an NFL team emblem on every bunch of Chiquita Bananas.

Now every time you buy a bunch, you get a team. Just peel them right off the peel. And collect them.

The faster you eat, the faster your collection grows.

And if you start eating now, by Super Bowl Day you may own the entire collection.

Good luck.

Chiquita is a registered trademark of United Fruit Company.

Chiquita Bananas, 1970

WISH-BONE.
FOR PEOPLE WHO REALLY LIKE SALADS.

People who love the natural goodness of fresh, crisp salad vegetables want only Wish-Bone. Because Wish-Bone dressings are perfectly balanced and blended to make every flavor taste as bright and lively as nature's good greens themselves. Wish-Bone. For people who really like salads.

-Bone Italian Dressing, 1973

Cream of the crop.

It's fresh as a country garden. Naturally delicious with the delicate flavor of real cucumber and rich sour cream. Chopped onion and cracked black pepper. It's KRAFT Creamy Cucumber dressing.

KRAFT
One of the salad wonders of the world.

Kraft Cucumber Dressing, 1978

Make a better salad with Bac·Os and Avocado.

Slice into the buttery cool of a luscious California Avocado. Then bring on the Bac=Os. Their bacon-like flavor enhances every sort of salad. Nutlike, delicate avocados and crunchy Bac=Os. Savor their flavors in your next salad.

Os Imitation Bacon, 1978

A ONE-OF-A-KIND TASTE
From Two Great Salad Makers

With Hidden Valley Ranch® Original Buttermilk Salad Dressings and Best Foods® Real Mayonnaise, you can create a dressing that's deliciously different.

Just mix Hidden Valley Ranch with milk or buttermilk and, of course, Best Foods. Best Foods smooth, rich consistency makes your dressing creamy-good.

And because you make it up fresh, this unique dressing gives you flavor you just can't get from a bottle. So for livelier-tasting salads, try Hidden Valley Ranch and Best Foods.

Hidden Valley Ranch
Ranch

Best Foods
REAL Mayonnaise
32 FL. OZ. (1 QT.)

The Original Flavor Buttermilk Dressings
HIDDEN VALLEY RANCH
Nobody else has our secret recipe ...or our special taste.

Bring out the best in your salad.
BEST FOODS
Real Mayonnaise

© 1979 Best Foods, a Unit of CPC North America

Hidden Valley Ranch Dressing, 1979

293

Dogs love cheese

Introducing the nourishing new dog food with real cheese right in it.*

Does your dog like the flavor of cheese? Just go to the kitchen and get him a piece of cheese and you'll see for yourself. If he's like other dogs he'll love cheese. That's why we made new Ken-L Ration Cheese Flavored Burger.

It has real cheese right in it. And it's completely nourishing... with all the protein, all the minerals, all the vital nutrients your dog needs. Ken-L Ration Cheese Flavored Burger has cheese. And dogs love cheese.

Ken-L Ration Dog Food, 1971

Veterinarians prefer Ken-L Ration over all other canned dog foods.

In a nationwide survey, veterinarians preferred Ken-L Ration over any other canned dog food—and by 6 to 1 over the other leading canned food.

The survey shows that most vets prefer a completely balanced meat and grain diet like Ken-L Ration...for the carbohydrates, vitamins, minerals, and fiber that meat alone doesn't have.

When it comes to your dog's diet, listen to what the vets say—give your dog Ken-L Ration.

Ken-L Ration Dog Food, 1978

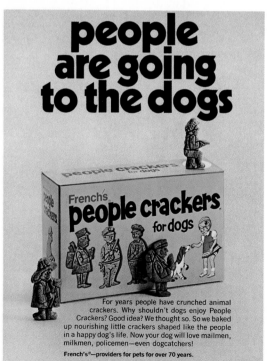

people are going to the dogs

For years people have crunched animal crackers. Why shouldn't dogs enjoy People Crackers? Good idea? We thought so. So we baked up nourishing little crackers shaped like the people in a happy dog's life. Now your dog will love mailmen, milkmen, policemen—even dogcatchers!

French's®—providers for pets for over 70 years.

French's People Crackers for Dogs, 1972

Coffee Time... **"I'd love a little snack too."**

When you have coffee, when the kids wangle cookies, how about a snack for me too? French's Doggie Do·Nuts, made just for dogs, like tiny bakery-fresh doughnuts—yet crisp and crunchy.
P.S. I also love French's® People Crackers. Regular or Liver-flavored.

French's Doggie Donuts, 1973

Ken-L Ration Dog Food, 1978

Interiors
296

LA-Z-BOY®

Relaxes All Kinds Of Dads!

for FATHER'S DAY

Because you love Dad, you want him to have the very best. No matter what kind of Dad he is — sportsman — TV buff — checker enthusiast or what, he will be pleased and happy in his La-Z-Boy reclining chair because it will give him the kind of comfort he has always wanted! And that includes real lay-back, stretch-out comfort.

Best news yet, Mom, **La-Z-Boy** reclining chairs are available in long-wearing, stain-resistant Herculon® Olefin Fibers, which are on sale now for Father's Day. No matter what the decor of the room — your La-Z-Boy dealer has the style for you.

Happy Father's Day, Dad!

On Sale Now At La-Z-Boy Dealers Everywhere!

Armstrong Floors, 1973 ◄ *La-Z-Boy Chairs, 1972*

► *Stroheim & Romann Fabrics, 1972*

Testing Bed & Testing Bureau designed By J. Wade Beam.

CASA BELLA

Casa Bella Furnishings, 1979

▶ *Pace Furniture, 1979*

310 LOUNGE CHAIR / DESIGN LEON ROSEN

pace®

Riviera Convertibles, 1974

Kroehler Furniture, 1974

Simmons Hide-A-Bed Sofa, 1973

Chatham Furniture, 1976

▶ Selig Furniture, 1974

when it's contempora[ry]

ARGOS © ORIGINAL EDWARD FIELDS DESIGN

when it's traditional ...

SHIRAZ © ORIGINAL EDWARD FIELDS DESIGN

NO LIMIT TO
CARPET
DESIGN AT / EDWARD FIELDS

NEW YORK 232 EAST 59TH ST. • LOS ANGELES 8950 BEVERLY B[LVD]

Van Luit & Co. Wallcoverings, 1972

Utica Fabrics, 1975

Edward Fields Rugs, 1972 ◄   *J. C. Penney Department Store, 1979*

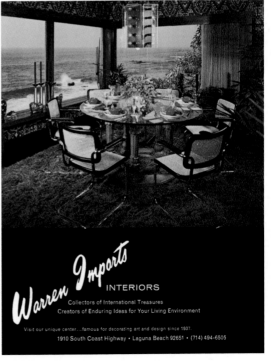

Warren Imports, 1972

Vectra®

Kroehler believes your furniture should be as generous and interesting as you are.

There's a welcome quality—a mood—to this Citation by Kroehler sofa that fits perfectly with the way you feel about people. It's a comfortable, sheltered nook for a very private conversation. And it loves to have a party!

Hotline: For your nearest Citation by Kroehler dealer, call 800-447-4700 toll free. (In Illinois: 800-322-4400.) For more decorating ideas, send for our 26-page full-color shopping guide: "Lively Living with Kroehler Furniture." Send 50¢ to: Kroehler Mfg. Co., Dept. I, 222 E. Fifth Street, Naperville, IL 60540.

79" Shelter Sofa (height of back: 39") with 2 Ottomans (each 38" long) in 100% Vectra® Olefin fibers: all 3 piece under $900. Also available as a Sleep-or-Lounge with luxurious queen-size (60 x 72") mattress. Sleep-or-Lounge with 2 Ottomans: under $1000. Manufacturer's suggested retail prices may vary by geographic area, an for fabrics other than shown. Upholstered pieces also available in other fashion fabrics protected with DuPont Zepel® stain repellent.

Citation by KROEHLER

STANLEY INTRODUCES FURNITURE FOR MS. VIRGINIA ALLEN.

Fresno, California

"I feel like Stanley knows us! Because their new Timbermist is so much like the way we feel about things. It's relaxed and kind of casual, but with a lot of style. And it's honest furniture, practical and sturdy, with oodles of storage and a soft finish that shows real respect for the wood.

But Timbermist is fun, too. I love the map drawer look and tambour doors. The neat accents of brass kick plates and pegged table tops. And the way it coordinates our living, dining, and bedrooms. Timbermist is a natural for us...made to last, comfortable to live with, and really reasonably priced. My husband and I have been asking for furniture like this. And Stanley heard us."

Manufacturer's suggested retail price for the storage headboard grouping shown is under $1,423. For a brochure on Timbermist, send $1.00 to: Stanley Furniture, Dept. 0K9; Stanleytown, Va. 24168.

Stanley Furniture
of Mead Company

Get something beautiful going at your place!

Dramatic, unconventional, practical "Gran Turismo." A striking contemporary bedroom with the European flair for chic style and functional design. Storage is everywhere. Shown here in dazzling white with polished chrome-finish

hardware, you can also get it in rich espresso brown. Conventional pieces such as five-drawer chests and triple dressers are also available. For folders of Lane furniture, send $1.00 to The Lane Co., Inc. Dept. N#12, Altavista, VA 24517.

Lane®
The Love Chest People

"Gran Turismo" is available at better furniture and department stores throughout the country.

Stanley Furniture, 1979

Lane Furniture, 1979

What nature started, we finish beautifully.

"Burlington Furniture is made slowly and carefully. Out of fine wood and wood veneers.

We take our time finishing our furniture. We hand sand, rub and wax it. We use up to 27 different hand-finishing processes. And we finish the parts you don't see as carefully as the parts you do see.

Take a look at our Vintage collection pictured here. It's made of fine oak solids and veneers. Construction features mortise and tenon joints, dovetailed drawers. The fine hardware is custom designed.

Most importantly, Burlington Furniture is created with you in mind by some of America's leading furniture designers. Be it dining room and bedroom, youth and modular furniture, colonial, traditional and contemporary designs.

Just look for Burlington Furniture wherever fine furniture is sold. Write to Burlington Furniture for further information, P.O. Box 907, Dept. B, Lexington, North Carolina 27292.

Burlington Furniture
A division of Burlington Industries.

Kroehler Furniture, 1975 ◄

Burlington Furniture, 1979

Feel clean all over

It's a grand feeling when everything's clean.
Rugs, walls, table tops, everything. And one of your
best helpers is gas heat. There's no heat cleaner
than gas. No heat more comfortable or dependable.
And do you know how thrifty gas heat is? Check into it—
with your gas company or heating contractor.

Gas heat gives you a better deal.

Chromcraft Furniture, 1974

Georgia-Pacific Paneling, 1970

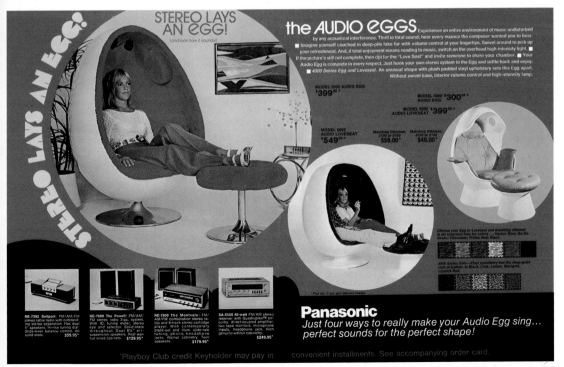

American Gas Association, 1971 ◄   *Panasonic Audio Egg, 1972*

▶ *Philadelphia Carpets, 1974*

SIGNATURES IN ACRIVUE

Mix it, match it, any way you turn it, UpDate turns you on.

Your bedrooms never came so alive! Just see what Bob Van Allen's new Up-Date collection can do for them! It's crafted by *Kenneth Home Fashions* into cozy comforters, wild bedspreads, gay dust ruffles, exciting draperies! Matching pillows and piece goods from Riverdale—treated with "Scotchgard" Brand Fabric Protector. Use all the same pattern, or mix them up.

There are four to choose from, and four colors: seafoam, earth, cadet blue, cranberry. All in a perfect blend of 50% Fortrel polyester, 50% cotton—machine washable. UpDate...what a wonderful way to sleep! What a wonderful way to decorate too—only from *Kenneth Home Fashions*. And so outstanding in fashion and value, they're a Celanese House selection.

Fortrel® is a trademark of Fiber Industries, Inc., a subsidiary of Celanese Corporation.

Selected patterns and colors available at fine stores everywhere.

Celanese House, 1977

TONIGHT.
We've spent 130 years getting your bed ready for it.

Butterflies are fresh when Dior does them. This is 'Delicado,' Wamsutta's latest contribution to the great contemporary bedroom. Yet the real beauty of these bed linens is behind the scenes. In the care and craftsmanship that went into their making. Something Wamsutta has been doing for 130 years. And the more we care, the less you have to. These sheets are made of a very soft, no-iron blend of Fortrel® polyester and cotton. Naturally, great design and quality are a continuing part of Wamsutta tradition. However, we'd hardly call ourselves traditional.

Wamsutta
Div. M. Lowenstein & Sons.
111 W. 40th St. N.Y.

Wamsutta, 1977

"smile" It's easier with Kodel®

Bloomcraft brings you bedroom eloquence. With an ensemble that says it dramatically...beautifully. This sophisticated "Wings" pattern in a blend of Kodel polyester and rayon can inspire your imagination to flights of fancy. Like the innovative way the pinch pleated draperies are used as a backdrop for the bed. And you'll fancy the soft bedspread quilted with KodOfill™ polyester fiberfill for sumptuous plumpness. Smile. Kodel helps keep it looking fresh morning after morning, night after night. Included in this collection are: standard size bedspreads, shams, 84" and 90" draperies. In the colors shown. At fine stores including those listed on the opposite page.

Bedroom ensemble by Bloomcraft. Kodel® polyester by Eastman.

EASTMAN CHEMICAL PRODUCTS, INC., a subsidiary of Eastman Kodak Company, 1133 AVENUE OF THE AMERICAS, NEW YORK, N.Y. 10036. KODEL is Eastman's trademark for its polyester fiber. Eastman does not make fabrics or consumer textile products and therefore makes no warranties with respect to such products.

1880 1980

The Swedlow Group Furniture, 1979 ◄   *Bloomcraft, 1979*

MARTEX. WE DESIGN FABRICS THAT HAPPEN TO BE SHEETS.

Here, "Summer Palace" joins two ancient Chinese traditions—hand painting and geometry—to make an exquisite contemporary bed. A bed that creates its own subtle atmosphere. Serene. Composed. Why not see what happens when you make your bed with Martex? Sheets and pillowcases of 50% Dacron® polyester/50% combed cotton. Also comforters, tailored petticoats, tailored shams, shower curtains and towels.

Detail from "Summer Palace" approximately 1/2 size.

MARTEX
LET US MAKE YOUR BED.

Martex Sheets, 1979

BURLINGTON "NIGHT FASHIONS"

Burlington creates alluring visions of medieval tapestries and castle gardens with "Madrigal," a new scenic design. Sheets and pillowcases are in luxurious Percale of 50% Combed cotton, 50% Kodel polyester. Bedspreads, draperies and towels accompany Burlington. So much to trust.
Available at fine stores everywhere. For the store nearest you, call this toll-free number anytime: 800-243-6000 (in Conn. call 1-800-882-6500).

"Madrigal" by The Burlington Design Studio

Night Venture:
Embroidery;
Hankies:
Monogrammed;
Stitch: Satin

KODEL®
Kodel® is a T.M. of the Eastman Kodak Co.

Burlington
BURLINGTON DOMESTICS, A DIVISION OF BURLINGTON INDUSTRIES, INC. NEW YORK, N.Y. 10019

Burlington Fabrics, 1977

▶ *Sears Department Store, 1973*

What puts the life in the World Trade Center?

Its size.
Its international scope.
Its view of the world.
Its wool-covered floors, partitions, chairs, even cabinet doors.

Never has a greater architectural project been undertaken—and never has wool been called upon to do so big a job. The World Trade Center rises 110 stories. Each of its twin towers is 1,350 feet high. It will have 9,000,000 square feet of office space upon completion. Each tower floor is an acre in size. And the carpeting is wool, of course.

The idea of a World Trade Center was born in 1960 when the business community of lower Manhattan recognized the need for such a business complex. In 1962, the Port Authority of New York and New Jersey was authorized by both States to develop the idea. Minoru Yamasaki and Associates and Emery Roth and Sons were commissioned architects. In 1966, ground was broken and on April 4, 1973, the formal dedication ceremony was held. One of the biggest architectural projects in the world is taking shape—a complex which includes the twin towers, the Customs House, the two Plaza buildings, and a proposed hotel.

Of course, tenants haven't waited for completion, and neither have their interior designers and carpet suppliers.

More than twenty-five of the World Trade Center's acres have been covered in wool, but for more wool acreage is projected.

The use of wool in the Trade Center might be described as three-faceted, with three classifications of areas to be covered. First, public areas including entrance lobbies, hallways, elevators and "skylobbies" or changeover points from local and express elevators on the forty-fourth and seventy-eighth floors. Second, the twenty-two Port Authority floors including executive offices, dining rooms and cafeterias, the World Trade Institute's language school and seminar rooms, the library, etc. Third, tenant areas.

This means that almost everywhere in the World Trade Center, wool warms concrete, cuts sun glare at windows, softens the sound of hundreds of thousands of phones, voices, footsteps. It adds flowing elegance, color, warmth, helping create a more human scale and ambience in these larger-than-life towers of concrete, steel and glass.

However, there was no need to review all these virtues when the time came to make a decision on carpet fiber. The decision was automatic. Fire Department regulations practically specified it.

Wool Bureau, 1974

SIMMONS.
10-month, turnkey package.
O'Hare International Tower Hotel.

Interior design: Norman de Haan, A.I.D., Norman de Haan Associates, Inc. Architect: C. F. Murphy Associates

Only Simmons could put together a package deal like this one—from conception to installation in just 10 months.

In April of 1972, Norman de Haan Associates, Inc., were brought in by Madison Square Garden Corporation to create the interiors of the new O'Hare International Tower Hotel. When plans were finished, in an incredibly short 8 weeks, all guestroom furnishings had been custom designed.

Simmons made them all. Delivered them on time. And worked out a tight installation timetable that allowed the hotel to open in February of 1973, just 10 months from project start.

The Tower presented unusual problems that demanded unusual custom solutions. Noise level was a big one. Simmons helped to solve it with sound-absorbent draperies from Bloomcraft. Carpeting has thick padding as part of the sound-control measures. And all furnishings meet the new flammability standards.

The 981 guestrooms have five carpet colors and six alternate Bloomcraft bedspread and drapery schemes, a tricky record-keeping challenge that Simmons handled without a hitch.

The unusual shape of the building, plus the need for a given number of rooms, made each room relatively small. Headboards with attached lights from Raymor/Richards, Morgenthau that also serve as bedside tables maximize the floorspace. Beds are on easily maintained plinth bases that conserve space. And all bedding is Beautyrest by Simmons.

Thonet created the sleek guestroom case goods. The handsome chairs are by Simmons Living Room Division. Both custom-designed by Norman de Haan, A.I.D. Much of the seating in public areas is from Selig and Thonet.

The lobby is rather long and narrow with glass walls on two sides. Mr. de Haan visually stretched the area with low profile Thonet fiberglass chairs and a Simmons geometric carpet spread throughout the entire area.

In addition there are 63 conference rooms, 18 meeting/banquet rooms, a mezzanine and seven restaurants. Furnished and accessorized for the most part with Simmons products.

The entire interior installation was coordinated by Simmons. It was done in vertical thirds as each section of the hotel was completed, making warehousing, delivery and scheduling of installation operations critical.

Remarkably, it all came together on time. And, Simmons can tailor a complete turnkey package for you.

With all the Simmons resources at your command, you save time as well as make pricing, coordination and installation immensely simpler.

Call Bob Costello, General Manager, Simmons Contract. (312) 644-4060. For a package plan par excellence.

Simmons Furniture, 1974

Boussac of France Inc.
Fabrics
979 Third Avenue · New York 10022 · 212·4210534
Showrooms in - Los Angeles, Miami, Seattle, Dallas,
Boston, San Francisco, Minneapolis, Chicago, Houston, Paris, London.
Richard Giglio

Boussac of France Fabrics, 1974

▸ Roman Shades by Ray, 1972 ▸▸ Eljer Plumbingware, 1972

The Pine Line. A lounge group with nothing between you and the honesty of its natural wood. Elemental. Adaptable. And most comfortable. The random width pine planks enclose plump urethane cubes. Chair, two and three seaters in your choice of fabrics. Complementary tables also available. See it at the Thonet Center of Design. New York. Chicago. Los Angeles. Dallas. Or write Thonet Industries Inc., 491 East Princess Street, York, Pa. 17405. Telephone (717) 845-6666.

THONET
CENTER OF DESIGN

Travel
324

Picking an airline for its food is like picking a restaurant for its flying ability.

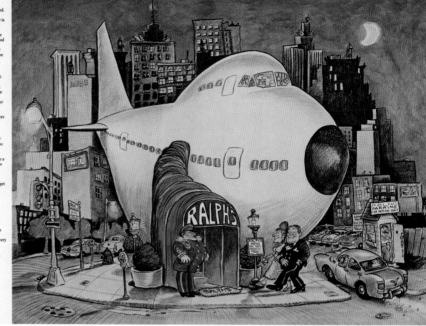

We don't know of a single restaurant that advertises itself as a great airline. Which is understandable.

However we do know of several airlines that advertise themselves as great restaurants. Which is absurd.

For no matter what an airline does (and none do more than we do) the closest it can come to great cuisine is good cuisine. The limitations of serving food at 30,000 feet see to that.

But that isn't the point. The point is, you don't get on an airplane to eat in the first place. No matter how good the food is. You get on an airplane to go somewhere.

And if that somewhere happens to be over 3,000 miles of ocean to a place you've never been, you need more than a pleasant plane ride.

You need help and advice before you leave.

If you've traveled a lot you know that planning things out thoroughly, before you leave, can mean the difference between a so-so vacation and a great vacation.

Over 7,000 Pan Am travel agents, all across the country, have the knowledge and experience to make sure yours is the latter. From a complete Pan Am tour (having invented the air tour, we offer a wider selection to more countries than anyone) to simply making air and hotel reservations for you wherever you're going.

In addition, there are more than 90 Pan Am offices in the U.S. alone, staffed with people willing and able to help you with everything from what to pack to where to stay. Or where not to.

You may need help and advice once you're there.

There's one thing you can always expect when you travel. The unexpected.

You run a little short of cash. You don't receive your mail from home. You want to change plans. If you're a Pan Am ticket holder you can walk into any of our offices throughout the world and get help with the unexpected.

You can cash a personal check in an emergency, arrange to pick up your mail through our special "Postal Service," change hotel or flight reservations and get assistance on other problems that may come up.

And you don't pay us anything extra for any of these services. The pre-trip planning or the help you get once you're there. Further, your air fare on Pan Am is no more than it is on any other scheduled airline.

There's one other thing you don't pay extra for at Pan Am.

Our experience.

We've opened more of the world to air travel than all other airlines combined.

We've introduced (and helped design) virtually every major commercial aircraft of the last 40 years. Including the 747.

Our experience and knowledge is so vast, in fact, that last year alone, 17 of the world's airlines sent their pilots and crews to us for advanced training.

Come to think of it, 7 airlines had us prepare a good share of the meals they served aboard.

Pan Am
The world's most experienced airline.

Pan Am Airlines, 1972

American Airlines New 747 LuxuryLiner.
The plane with no competition.

Coach Lounge.

First Class Lounge.

No matter where you've been in the world, you've never gone in comfort like this. From our spacious new Coach Lounge, with its stand-up bar, all through the plane and up the stairs, to our totally redesigned first class lounge. It's a new standard in flying comfort. The American Airlines 747 LuxuryLiner. First of all, in coach, there's a lounge bigger than most living rooms.

It's a place where you can mingle, make new friends, have a snack, have some fun. Enjoy being sociable, or just enjoy the space. No other airline has anything like it. And back down the aisle at your seat, we've rearranged the rows. So besides getting **more leg room and sitting room,** you'll have more getting up room when you try out the lounge. If you're flying first class, why not call ahead

and **reserve a table for four.** You can wine and dine with friends, do a little business, or maybe play some bridge. And a floor above is our beautiful new first class lounge. A plush, intimate spot where you can socialize over after-dinner liqueurs or champagne. And for everybody on transcontinental flights,

there's an added service. Flagship Service. Featuring Polynesian food. Special warming wagons to keep your food piping hot. And pretty new outfits for our stewardesses. So if you like going places to see things, this new airplane is something to see. Every one of our 747s is now a LuxuryLiner. And all of the extra comforts won't cost you an extra cent. For reservations call us or your Travel Agent.

American Airlines 747 LuxuryLiner

American Airlines, 1971 ◄ *American Airlines, 1971*　　　　　► *Pan Am Airlines, 1972*

A couple of tough customers. Ours.

Walt Frazier and Jerry Lucas of the New York Knickerbockers.

When the men of the National Basketball Association go out of town on business they expect to have a rough time.

But on the way to and from, they want things made easy.

United understands.

Maybe that's why all 17 NBA teams fly United to away games. And, in fact, why we fly more pro and college sports teams than any other airline.

Because we don't play games with them.

These guys are travel pros, too. They want convenience, attention, service, without asking. And in the friendly skies, they've got it.

United knows that business people come in all shapes and styles. So we take them one at a time. And make things easy for all of them. Each in his own way.

The next time you're going out of town, call your Travel Agent, or United.

And say you're a tough customer. We'll take you on, too.

The friendly skies of your land
United Air Lines
Partners in Travel with Western International Hotels.

United Airlines, 1973

NOW, A WHOLE NEW WAY TO FLY ACROSS THE UNITED STATES. TWA's NEW AMBASSADOR SERVICE.

If you've suffered through a five hour flight, eating dull food, watching a movie you've already seen, we've got news for you.

TWA's new Ambassador Service.

Everything starts at the front of the terminal. The Skycap takes your bags. You head straight for the gate.

Where you find our new Ground Ambassador. If you have any problem, that's why he's there.

On board, you'll find new colors, new carpet, new seats, more room, better everything.

Especially in coach. Where we ripped the old seats out of our 707's. And put in our new Twin Seats.

You'll find a choice of 3 International meals in coach, 5 in first class. With champagnes, wines and liqueurs from around the world.

After dinner, sit back, and we bring on the entertainment. Eight channels of stereo music, humor and news. And on every movie flight, a choice of two movies!

When you land, you may find your bags waiting for you for a change. We've put in a whole new, faster baggage system.

Next time you're flying across the United States, take a TWA 707 or 747 Ambassador Flight. It's a whole new way to fly.

TWA Airlines, 1970

WHAT TWA DID FOR COACH... TWA NOW DOES FOR 1ST CLASS.

Last Fall TWA introduced Ambassador Service, a whole new way to fly for the coach passenger.

There's the new Twin Seat. If the plane's not crowded, it can be three across, two across or even a couch.

You'll find a choice of three international meals. With wines, champagnes and liqueurs from around the world!

You'll find a choice of two movies on every movie flight! One for general audiences, one for mature.

You'll find new carpets, new colors, new fabrics, new hostess uniforms, new everything.

The only problem was, first class started to look dull by comparison, so...

TWA's NEW AMBASSADOR SERVICE.

...we took out those old overstuffed first class seats.

And put in all new overstuffed first class seats.

We put in a choice of five meals, the best you'll find on any airline, anywhere.

After dinner, settle back, and we present a choice of two movies on every movie flight. One for general audiences, one for mature.

And on top of this (and below it and all around it) you'll find new colors, new carpets, new fabrics, new everything.

Next time you're flying to Boston, Hartford, New York, Newark, Philadelphia, Baltimore, Washington, Columbus, Cincinnati or Chicago take a TWA 707 or 747 Ambassador Flight.

Coach or first class, nobody else gives you anything like it.

TWA's NEW AMBASSADOR SERVICE.

TWA Airlines, 1971

▶ *Northstar Ski Resort, 1972* ▶▶ *Western Airlines, 1970*

329

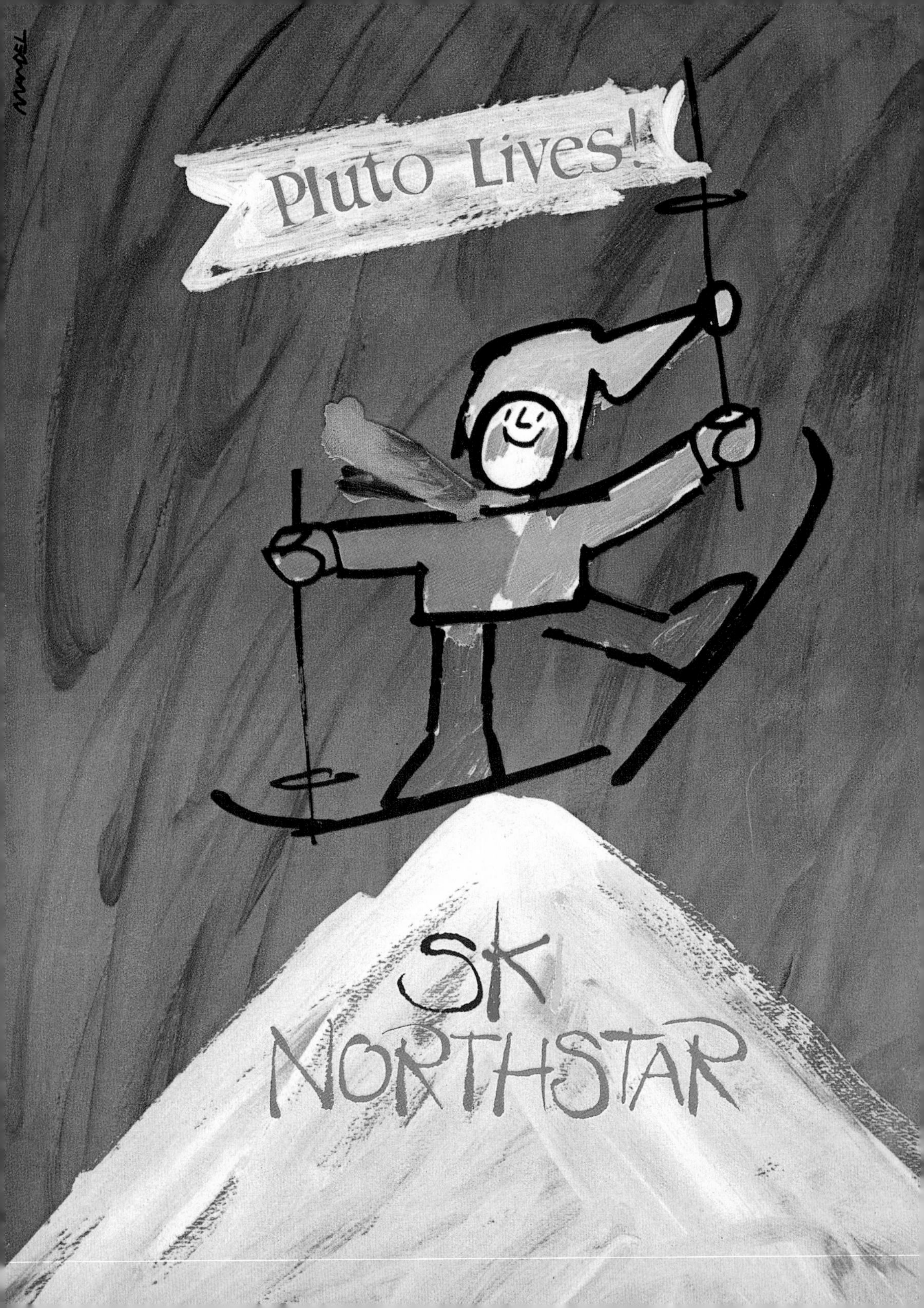
MANDEL
Pluto Lives!
SKI
NORTHSTAR

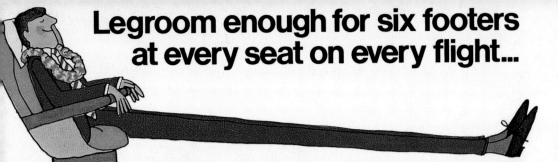

Legroom enough for six footers at every seat on every flight...

just part of Western's service to Hawaii

Welcome aboard the "Islander," where you'll enjoy First Class comfort at Coach fares. It's our "Deluxe Coach" with plenty of stretch-out legroom, because all seats in Coach and Economy are spaced exactly the same as First Class. And when the number of passengers permits, Western's ingenious "Aloha Table" gives you Two + Two seating—with First Class width, too. If you think "Deluxe Coach" sounds great, wait 'til you see how we pamper you in First Class!

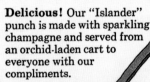

Delicious! Our "Islander" punch is made with sparkling champagne and served from an orchid-laden cart to everyone with our compliments.

Feast "Islander" style. With your choice of gourmet entrees in both Coach and First Class. And special Economy meal service at minimal cost. It's all served up by stewardesses in the latest Hawaiian fashion— the mini-muumuu. Plus an Executive Hostess— your inflight expert.

Featuring: wide screen movies and a choice of six stereo channels for your pleasure.

Be a winner! You may win a prize that will remind you of Hawaii and your "Islander" flight in our Inflight Sweepstakes.

WESTERN TO HAWAII
the _only_ way to fly

For reservations and information on low-cost tours, just ask your Travel Agent—he knows!

SCANDINAVIA. SHE'S MORE THAN YOU DREAMED.

NORWAY: Ancient Viking Ships. Majestic Fjords. A park that's a sculpture museum. Picturesque open air markets. Scenic railroad trips through the mountains. Unique Stave Churches. Unrivaled deep-sea and fresh water fishing.

DENMARK: Hans Christian Andersen Fairytale Villages. Hamlet's Castle. Tivoli Gardens. The Little Mermaid. The Royal Palace. Bicycling, Sailing, Swimming. Life-seeing.

SWEDEN: Skansen, the outdoor live folk museum. The beautiful ride through the Gota Canal. Stockholm and its 30,000 Islands. Lappland's picturesque people, unchanged in centuries. Dance Festivals under the Midnight Sun. Underground gourmet restaurants centuries old.

Scandinavian Tourist Board, 1974

italy
where hospitality is an art

The art of welcoming you in the universal language of her culture: masterpiece cities to be admired stone by stone, music, folklore, fine handicraft work.

The art of making you fall in love with her sunsets, her sparkling sea, her exquisite cuisine.

The art of making you feel at ease with the efficient services of a modern country: excel-

lent air, rail and sea connections, 2,800 miles of super highways, 35% discount on gasoline and free road service offered by ENIT and the Automobile Club, special railroad tourist rates, admission passes to all national museums, impeccable hotel organization. The art of making you smile with the warmth, the joy of living, that is so typically Italian.

For information
ITALIAN GOVERNMENT TRAVEL OFFICE (E.N.I.T.)
500 North Michigan Avenue · Chicago, Illinois 60611
630 Fifth Avenue · New York, N.Y. 10020
St. Francis Hotel, Post Street, San Francisco 94119 Cal.
3, Place Ville Marie, Suite 22 · Montreal 113 (Canada) and all travel Agencies.

Information request coupon
For free illustrative material on Italy, please send this coupon to the nearest ENIT office.
Name
Address
City _____ State _____
Specify the city or region in which you are particularly interested

Italian Government Travel Office, 1972

Weekend in a castle on the Rhine with your savings from Eurailpass.

Or enjoy 2 extra days in Paris. You can, with the money you save seeing Europe by train on Eurailpass—instead of driving.

Eurailpass is one rail ticket good for unlimited First Class travel in 15 countries. On fast, frequent, often luxurious trains. Sleep on a train, gain extra daylight hours for sight-seeing. Stop off if you like, at some intriguing spot, and go on later. Also get free or discount rides on many boats, ferries and buses.

All this at an unbeatable bargain. Unlimited First Class rail travel for 15 days, $190. 21 days, $230. One month, $280. Two months, $390. Three months, $460. And a Eurail Youthpass—for those under 26—2 months of Economy travel for $260.

One roundtrip can get you your money's worth. Paris to Vienna, say, is $601 on a typical 2-week car rental, $229 by regular First Class train, only $190 with a 15-day Eurailpass. For full details send for our booklet. **Note:** you can't buy Eurailpass in Europe. Buy it here from your Travel Agent.

EURAILPASS
Box Q
Staten Island, NY 10305   332A-219
Please send me all the information I need to see Eurailpass' Europe.
Name
Address
City _____ State _____ Zip

EURAILPASS
See Europe for Less.

EURAILPASS EUROPE: Austria, Belgium, Denmark, Finland, France, Germany, Greece, Italy, Luxembourg, Netherlands, Norway, Portugal, Spain, Sweden, Switzerland.

Eurailpass, 1979

HOW TO GET MORE MILEAGE OUT OF YOUR MONEY IN BRITAIN.

Take the train. Any way you figure it, the train is the best way to travel in Britain. And the more you travel,

the more you save. For example, a BritRail Pass bought here in the U.S. gives you unlimited Economy train travel for two weeks for $105. And there are lots more specials, from a money saving tour of Ireland to the SeaPass that saves on Channel crossings. But money isn't the only reason.

THE TRAIN TAKES YOU DIRECT TO THE HEART AND SOUL OF BRITAIN.

You're not getting the most out of your travels if you only see the country. It adds so much to meet the people. (After all, you didn't come all the way to Britain to meet Americans!)

Nothing beats the train for meeting the British. It's their favorite mode of travel. As the miles go clicking away, you'll find them relaxed and ready for chatting away. (There really are lovely people hiding behind those British newspapers!)

THE TRAIN TAKES YOU IN HIGH STYLE FOR A LOW PRICE.
You'll ride comfortably, dine deliciously and ride high at low cost.

THE TRAIN MAKES TRACKS ALL OVER BRITAIN.
You can save money on every mile, anywhere you go. From the Lake District to the Cotswolds and everything in between. And all within hours of London. You'll travel on crack inter-city express trains with first-

class dining cars (wine served, of course!) or lively locals that wind

through picturesque villages. (We even have a wonderful narrow-gauge steam train in Wales!) Plus cross-Channel boat service to

Ireland and Continental Europe.

THE TRAIN BOOKLET—FOR MORE MILEAGE.
We have a most informative full-color brochure called "Easy Guide to BritRail." It tells you more about train travel than we could do justice to in this limited

space. Mail the coupon for your free copy. For more information, call your Travel Agent or BritRail Travel. You'll find out why, when you come to Britain, it would be a shame to miss the train.

BritRail Travel
THE BEST WAY TO THE HEART OF BRITAIN
CIRCLE # 12 ON READER SERVICE PAGE.

BRITRAIL TRAVEL INTERNATIONAL
Box 5, Dept. 172-725
Staten Island, NY 10305
Please send me my free copy of "Easy Guide to BritRail."
Name
Address
City _____ State _____ Zip

BritRail Travel, 1979

► *Airstream Trailers, 1979*

The thousand-year-old airline.

We began, not with our 747 Garden Jets, but with a legend. The legend of the tsuru, a crane native to Japan, whose story is such that parents once told their children to "behave like the tsuru."

For us at Japan Air Lines, the truest motivation is still to "behave like the tsuru." To fly the highest and farthest like the tsuru, yes. But, more, to reflect the care, serenity, and courtesy which the tsuru symbolizes. To bring the legend to life.

Simple things like courtesy tend to get lost in the crowd of today. In the heritage of Japan, however, they are a matter of character, not ceremony. They have the force and authority of over a thousand years of commitment. At Japan Air Lines, we share that commitment. And the commitment is absolute.

JAPAN AIR LINES JAL

Japan Air Lines, 1971

JAL made it to the top by helping tourists know the Orient instead of merely looking at it.

On JAL's Happi Holidays tours of the Orient, you see a world where the sights aren't merely variations of the sights back home. Where wonders are commonplace. Where splendor is taken for granted.

Even more important, JAL's Orient is a place where you gather memories of the people you've met as well as the sights you've seen.

These are the reasons why more people tour the Orient with JAL than with any other airline.

Come to JAL's Orient. See your travel agent or send us the coupon today. And come this year, not next year or the year after. As an old Japanese proverb says, "Time flies like an arrow." Another suggests, "The day you decide to do a thing is the best day to do it."

We never forget how important you are.
JAPAN AIR LINES
Box 618, N.Y., N.Y. 10011
☐ Please send JAL's ORIENT booklet with complete tour listings and ORIENT TOUR BUYING GUIDE.
Name
Address_____City
State____Zip____Tel.
My Travel Agent_____Key #
RB 052278

Japan Air Lines, 1978

Now's the time to make a dream come true.

JAL's Orient. Mysterious and exotic, paradise and adventure, a multitude of cultures, customs, people and languages. It's all there for you to experience.

Come and watch Kabuki, a Japanese drama. Visit gilded palaces in Bangkok, admire ancient temples in Malaysia or just relax on one of Bali's beautiful beaches.

Now stop dreaming. JAL's Happi Holidays tours offer a variety of itineraries at prices that are lower than you may expect.

Choose one. You'll find it's the best way to make a dream come true.

For more information, see your travel agent or write Japan Air Lines, Dept. SU, P.O. Box 618, New York, N.Y. 10011

This year, the Orient.
JAPAN AIR LINES

Japan Air Lines, 1979

How to Fly, Japanese Style.

We once asked some of our flight guests what they liked most about flying with us. Surprisingly, it wasn't any of the comforts or delicacies above.

In fact, it wasn't what we did so much as how we did it.

They spoke of being pampered. Of the way our hostesses in kimono smile. Small things, of course. But in a world that worships the mammoth, the small has a way of making up in gleam what it lacks in size.

At JAL, we glory in the small things of life. From our first hello to our last sayonara, we take the small attentions and courtesies so much for granted, they are our way of life.

It's a way of life practiced by us and our ancestors of generations beyond number.

In that sense, you could say we've been practicing how to fly for a thousand years and more.

JAPAN AIR LINES

Japan Air Lines
P.O. Box 888
Burlingame, California 94010
I'd like to fly Japanese style. Please send me your free booklet with all the details.
Name
Address
City____State____Zip
My travel agent is
Please have a travel consultant call me at

Japan Air Lines, 1974

▶ Japan Air Lines, 1970

Costa Rica Tourist Board, 1978

Costa Rica Tourist Board, 1979

Mexican Government Tourist Office, 1979

Mexican Government Department of Tourism, 1972　▶ *Mexicana Airlines, 1972*

Mexico & Mexicana. We're the best things going.

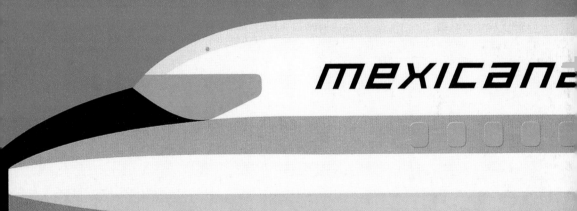

When you're going to Mexico, we'll give you the best thing going. Our luxurious Golden Aztec service. From 8 U.S. cities to all 20 of the best places going. So see your travel agent. Send this coupon. Or call us toll-free at 800-421-8301, (From California, 800-252-0251, toll-free. From L.A. 213-687-6950). And get going yourself.

Mexicana Airlines, P.O. Box 4249, Burlingame, CA 94010. I'd like to get going myself. Send me more information about your tours to:

☐ Cancun ☐ Cozumel ☐ Mexico City ☐ Puerto Vallarta ☐ Guadalajara ☐ Mazatlan ☐ Acapulco ☐ Other_____

Name_____ Address_____ City_____

State/Zip_____ My travel agent is_____

*NWSC18

The airline most people fly to Mexico.

U.S. Virgin Islands Information Center, 1970

Bahamas Islands Tourist Office, 1970

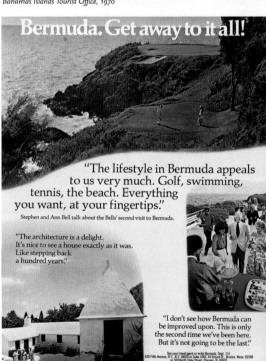

Bahamas Islands Tourist Office, 1979

Bermuda, 1979

...elegance epitomized by the resort
fashions Acapulco inspires. It's the
informal elegance your hostess
achieves at the little dinners
in her villa. It's the informal
elegance you enjoy in the resort's top restaurants
whether you dine on continental cuisine or Mexican
dishes. It's the informal elegance that keynotes
a moonlit midnight cruise of the bay. It's the informal
elegance of the dancing at the discotheques
that dawn discovers. Recapture the
elegance of Acapulco. Make it
a point to do it soon.

MEXICO
THE *Amigo* COUNTRY.

ecretaria de Turismo • Consejo Nacional de Turismo

sort fashions by Halston photographed
Nadine Markova during Three Evenings to
member in Acapulco sponsored by Braniff
ernational Airways, Secretaria de Turismo and the
xican National Tourist Council

Mexico Secretary of Tourism, 1977

▶ *Great Western Cities, 1970*   ▶▶ *Memphis Chamber of Commerce, 1971*

FREE !

Win an all-expense paid vacation for two in

HAWAII SWEEPSTAKES

Enter the
GREAT WESTERN CITIES

Travel to Hawaii on one of CONTINENTAL AIRLINES' luxurious Golden Hawaiian Flights

WIN one of our FREE HAWAIIAN VACATIONS for two!

(Three all-expense paid vacations for two via Continental Airlines.)

Or one of the 10,000 FREE vacations in beautiful California City in sunny Southern California. (Food and transportation not included.) FREE lodging, entertainment and unlimited use of recreation facilities.

Please enter my name in the Great Western Cities Inc. Sweepstakes. I assume no obligation by entering this contest.

NAME (Please Print)_____

ADDRESS_____

CITY_____ STATE _____ ZIP_____

AGE_____ OCCUPATION_____ **W 1-4**

This Sweepstakes is for people who like to travel and do exciting things . . . We want you to know about California City . . . the fabulous new vacationland city of the future in Antelope Valley.

OFFICIAL RULES:

1. This entire coupon must be cut out on dotted line or a reasonable facsimile in approximately the same size must be hand drawn and mailed.
2. Complete the entry coupon and mail to: Great Western Cities Incorporated, 6363 Sunset Boulevard, Los Angeles, California 90028.
3. Entries must be postmarked no later than January 31, 1970.
4. Sweepstakes limited to persons 21 years or older.
5. Winners will be determined by random drawings. Drawings will be conducted by an independent judging organization on March 31, 1970. Winners will be notified by mail. One prize per family.
6. Employees and their families of Great Western Cities Inc., their advertising and contest agencies are not eligible. No purchase required. Void where prohibited by law for any reason. All federal, state, and local regulations apply.

Memphis is ready for take-off. Come soar with us. You'll like our style, because we're looking for the same thing you are: expansion. What's more, the very assets that make us look good are the ones that will mean profit and growth for your company in Memphis.

Memphis has big-city production capabilities: manpower, land, low utility rates, location, and fine transportation facilities. Big-city office space, too. And we offer all this without big-city problems. As Memphis grows bigger, it grows better —carefully maintaining a friendly, relaxed way of life.

If you'd like the best of two worlds for your people, write on your company letterhead to **Dan Dale**, Director of Industrial Development, Memphis Light, Gas and Water, Box 388C, or **Ralph U. Thomas**, Mgr., Economic Development Dept., Memphis Area Chamber of Commerce, Box 224R, Memphis, Tennessee 38101.

MEMPHIS
CITY OF MANAGEABLE SIZE

Tahiti is getting
away from it all...
or to it all.

Peace On Earth

We grew up in a world of blue skies and lazy afternoons.

Look out almost any window and you'll see flowering plumeria, hibiscus and orchids, growing wild in the yard. The way dandelions might grow in yours. This is our South Pacific. And we'd like to take you there.

We'll show you the magical places that Michener and Maugham wrote about. The colors that Gauguin spent half a lifetime trying to capture.

We'll take you to Tahiti, where the first language is smiles and the second is French.

You'll picnic on deserted coves by a crystal clear ocean. And scuba dive where fish aren't fish at all, but underwater peacocks.

If you can get away from telephones and time clocks for just 10 days, we'll help you escape to Tahiti for as little as $745.*

Or we'll whisk you away to Fiji, the friendliest of all the islands. Or Rarotonga, the most unspoiled paradise of all.

Our luxurious DC-10s fly to the wonders of the South Pacific from Los Angeles.

Call your travel agent. Those Tahitian sunsets are waiting.

*GIT airfare, per person double occupancy.

Air New Zealand, 1978

Raiatea. This is the birthplace of Polynesian culture. On Saturday night, you can meet the population of the whole island. When they all come into town for one big party.

Huahine. This was the center of the Polynesian religion. You'll see an open-air museum with recently restored ruins of 400-year old temples that we call maraes.

Rangiroa. You can dive or snorkel all day in one of the world's largest lagoons. It's 22 miles long. You can even catch your own lobster and learn to paddle an outrigger canoe.

Bora Bora. This little island is almost completely surrounded by a barrier reef where you'll see some of the most spectacular coral formations in the world.

Tahiti and Moorea. Two of the most delightful islands in the whole South Pacific. Complete with luxury hotel suites, French, Polynesian, Chinese and American cuisine, and acres and acres of pure peace and quiet.

SOMEDAY, YOU'LL ESCAPE TO TAHI AND THAT'S ONLY THE BEGINNIN

Right now, Tahiti probably seems like everything could ask for. It has craggy mountains, blue lagoons, golder beaches, French restaurants, torchlit feasts and the most gen fun-loving people in the world. We Tahitians.

What more could you want out of life? You'll find soon enough. Because after you've seen Tahiti, that's only th beginning. There's Moorea with Cook's Bay, which is probal the most photographed spot in the South Pacific. There's Bo Bora. Which James Michener called "the most beautiful islan the world." And Raiatea. Where you can still see our ancient Polynesian fire-walking ceremonies. And Huahine. Where you step back 400 years by visiting the outdoor temples where ou ancestors worshipped. And Rangiroa. Where you can scuba in a 22 mile-long lagoon.

If you've always wanted to come to Tahiti, this is year to come. Because now there's so much more Tahiti to s Write us for vacation facts. Tahiti Tourist Board, P.O. Box 3 Hollywood, CA. 90028, Dept. 203.

Tahiti Tourist Board, 1970 ◄

Tahiti Tourist Board, 1974

If You Like To Cut Up!

Visit *Las Vegas*

call your travel agent!

A Las Vegas Convention Authority Advertisement.

Las Vegas Convention Authority, 1973

▶ *Las Vegas Convention Authority, 1973*

LAS VEGAS

Waiting just over the horizon is a dream vacation of top entertainment, delicious dining, excellent hotel and motel accommodations, all at a moderate cost. Las Vegas is a 24 hour town of sophisticated indoor fun and offers 12 full months of outdoor recreation, ranging from frosty ski slopes at 12,000 foot Mt. Charleston to sunny shores on sparkling Lake Mead. Tennis, golf, fishing, water skiing, horseback riding and swimming complete the Las Vegas sports picture. Downtown Las Vegas, the most photographed street in the world, is a million volt valley of light, brightening the midnight sky, and the famous "Strip" sparkles like a silver ribbon through the moonlit Nevada desert. See Las Vegas, the entertainment capitol of the world...your travel agent can get you in the act. Call him today!

THE MEETING PLACE

Meet at night. In Club Cerromar for dinner, dancing and a fabulous nightclub show. Or dine in the candlelit Surf Room. Get together later at the elegant Casino or for an after dinner drink (and more dancing) at the El Yunque. Meet in the bright, warm sun. On the golden, crescent beach. Play a brisk set or two on one of the 13 all-weather tennis courts. Putt for pars on the perfectly groomed, emerald greens of our two splendid Robert Trent Jones golf courses. Meet in the shade. At the thatched, open-air bar by the pool. Or on the balcony of your room overlooking the sparkling sea. Meet early for breakfast at the magnificent buffet on the Ocean Terrace. Meet late in the swinging discotheque. And, of course, meet to meet. In our Grand Salon. One of the most magnificent convention ballrooms in the world. Use live talent on our fully-equipped stage. Mount a multi-screen extravaganza. Or gather in one of the seminar rooms. They're perfect for small groups. The Cerromar Beach Hotel. Part of the gracious world of Regent International. At Dorado Beach, Puerto Rico. A tropical paradise where you'll want to meet again and again. For business. For pleasure. Your travel agent will make reservations for you. Or call LRI. Or Regent International toll-free at:
800-421-0530 Nationwide
800-252-0277 California
213-652-1454 Los Angeles.

CERROMAR BEACH HOTEL

Cerromar Beach Hotel, 1978

Sheraton...
Right on Waikiki Beach.

You're going too far to settle for less.

Waikiki Beach is the center of Hawaiian fun and excitement. And Sheraton has four luxury resort hotels right on Waikiki Beach. A fifth Sheraton is a half block away.

Sheraton offers a wide range of accommodations to suit your budget — from beautiful mountain-view rooms at the Princess Kaiulani for just $20.00* double occupancy, to sumptuous oceanfront Tower rooms at the Royal Hawaiian for $52.00.*

For reservations and complete information see your travel agent or call Sheraton at this toll-fre

800-325-3535

And don't miss Sheraton's delightful Neighbor Island hotels: Sheraton-Maui on Kaanapali Beach and Sheraton-Kauai on Poipu Beach.

* $23.00 to $57.00 February-March

Princess Kaiulani
(a half block from the beach)

Moana
Surfrider

Royal
Hawaiian

Sheraton-Waikiki

Stay at one Sheraton, play and charge at all five.

Sheraton Hotels in Hawaii
SHERATON HOTELS & MOTOR INNS, WORLDWIDE
P.O. BOX 8559, HONOLULU, HAWAII 96815   808/922-4422

In Chicago, Hyatt's a 700-foot column of Oriental kites rising through spanning bridges and hanging gardens. In Atlanta, Hyatt's glass bubble elevators glide through a park 24 stories tall.

In Knoxville, Hyatt's an Aztec pyramid. In Toronto, a tower of shimmering glass.

Hyatt's got butler service in San Francisco. A lounge that orbits Houston. The largest swimming pool in Acapulco.

And the toll free number gets you information and reservations at any Hyatt Hotel. Call your Travel Agent. Or Hyatt. And get it all.

HYATT HOTELS

800-228-9000 GetsYou Hyatt

Hyatt Hotels, 1975

Hotel Inter-Continental, 1978

Hyatt Hotels, 1972 ◄

Desert Inn, 1978

Index

Imprint

To stay informed about upcoming TASCHEN titles, please
request our magazine at www.taschen.com/magazine or
write to TASCHEN, Hohenzollernring 53, D–50672 Cologne,
Germany, contact@taschen.com, Fax: +49–221–254919. We
will be happy to send you a free copy of our magazine which
is filled with information about all of our books.

Art direction & design: Jim Heimann, L.A.
Digital composition & design: Cindy Vance, Modern Art &
Design, L.A.
Cover design: Sense/Net, Andy Disl and Birgit Reber,
Cologne
Production: Tina Ciborowius, Cologne
Project management: Sonja Altmeppen, Cologne
German translation: Anke Caroline Burger, Berlin
French translation: Philippe Safavi, Paris
Spanish translation: Gemma Deza Guil for LocTeam, S.L.,
Barcelona

Printed in China
ISBN 3–8228–5081–0